HAWAII: FIFTIETH STATE

by the author of

OCEANIA

HE SAILED WITH CAPTAIN COOK

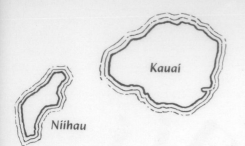

Niihau

Kauai

Oahu

HONOLULU ★

Hawaii

...FIFTIETH STATE

by Charles A. Borden

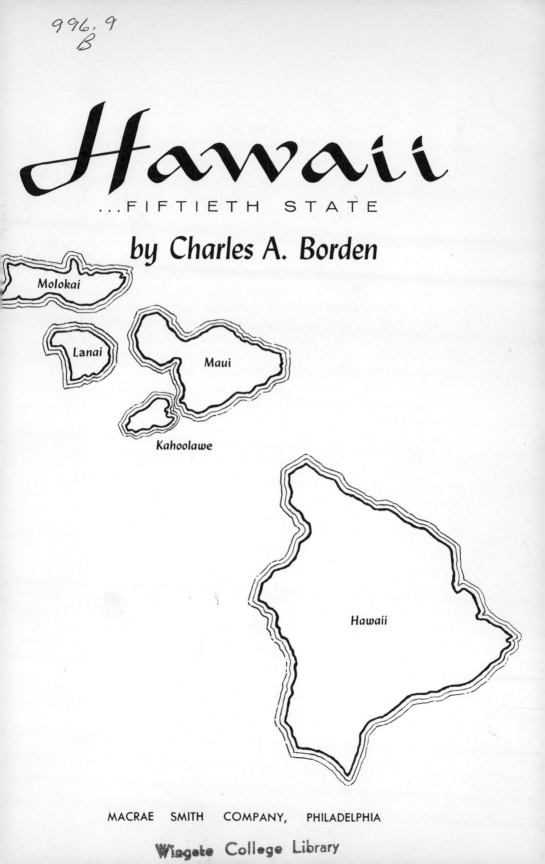

Molokai

Lanai

Maui

Kahoolawe

Hawaii

MACRAE SMITH COMPANY, PHILADELPHIA

ACKNOWLEDGMENTS

The author wishes to thank the following for permission to reproduce photographs in this book: American Factors, p. 134; Archives of Hawaii, pp. 73, 76, 84, 106; Brown of Honolulu, p. 136; California and Hawaiian Sugar Company, pp. 38, 100, 118, 140, 143; Castle and Cook, p. 132; Dole Photo, pp. 111, 147, 151; Hawaiian State Fish and Game Division, p. 61; Hawaii Visitors Bureau, pp. 12, 17, 22, 28 (Scoop Tsuzuki, photographer), 31, 40, 50, 54, 70, 81, 103, 154, 167; Honolulu Academy of Arts, p. 87; Kamehameha Schools, pp. 15, 166; Matson Lines, pp. 20, 57, 62, 63 (right); Pan American World Airways, p. 63 (left); Photo Hawaii, p. 156; United Air Lines, p. 176; United States Navy, p. 121; William V. Ward, p. 139; R. Wenkam, pp. 45, 162, 163, 172. Title page map and map on p. 35 by Guy Fry.

FOR Eleanor Dixon

Contents

HAWAII: FIFTIETH STATE

Chapter one

HAWAII TODAY: THE PEOPLE

"*H*AWAII NO KA OY—THERE'S NO PLACE LIKE HAWAII," THE Polynesians once said. Mark Twain called it "the loveliest fleet of islands that lie anchored in any sea." Today the Islanders proudly maintain that there's no place like Hawaii, the Fiftieth State.

Democracy and the spirit of Hawaii have blended well. Today, people from many countries of the Pacific live, work and mingle together in Hawaii just as people from Europe and other countries have done on our Atlantic Coast.

The Governor of the "Island State" is an Irishman from Missouri, the Attorney General is Japanese, the Senate President is Chinese and the Mayor of Honolulu is part Hawaiian. People of many different colors and backgrounds have achieved harmony and a satisfactory way of life within the modern Island setting.

The most numerous people are the Japanese, who in 1959 made up thirty-two percent of the population. They are followed, in descending order, by thirty percent white Caucasians, seventeen percent part-Hawaiian, eleven percent Filipinos and six percent Chinese. The dwindling population of pure Hawaiians, Puerto Ricans, Koreans, Portuguese and a sprinkling of other races comprise the rest.

When you say "the Hawaiians" you are speaking properly of all the people who live on the Islands. But when Islanders say the

These girls in front of the Myohoji Mission, a Honolulu Buddhist temple, are of Chinese, Japanese, Caucasian, Korean and Cosmopolitan (mixed) ancestry.

Hawaiians they mean only the pure Polynesian Hawaiians who comprise but two percent of the state's 625,000 population.

Young people born in Hawaii, regardless of their racial background, are American citizens. They speak English, go to modern American schools and do the things that most Americans do. The sons and daughters as well as the grandsons and granddaughters of Chinese and Japanese are as well educated, as ambitious, as filled with American ideals as the young descendants of those who came to Plymouth on the Mayflower.

Boys and girls in Hawaiian schools use many of the same books that are used in schools throughout the United States. They talk about the same things and play many of the same games, and are vitally interested in topics that interest young people in San Francisco, Kansas City or Philadelphia.

Education has always been popular in Hawaii. Among the people of Oriental or mixed background, most of whose parents or grandparents were plantation workers, education is a cherished privilege. They are determined to avoid going back to the "ko-hana," hard physical work, of their fathers and grandfathers. They study seriously and intensely. Hundreds are college graduates and have gone on to become teachers, engineers, lawyers, doctors and senators. Perhaps some day an Island-born son will become Governor, or even President of the United States.

Students from all over the Pacific are enrolled at the University of Hawaii. They study many things, including such vital Hawaiian subjects as volcanoes and fruit flies. The campus is like a small international city. Over twenty-one hundred cars arrive daily to try to park in the school's eleven hundred parking spaces. Surrounded by the sea, the University has courses on reefs, ocean depths, fish, currents, tidal waves and typhoons. Special studies are being made of fish dispersal and shark repellents, and on the transfer of radioactivity from fish to humans. The College of Arts and Sciences offers thirty courses in music, and courses in the sciences are heavily attended. Large classes studying the cultures of the Far East reveal that these students are years ahead of those in mainland schools in their awareness of the importance of the Orient and the need for a deeper understanding of its people. Most Hawaiian students feel that they have a great stake in the future of the United States in the Pacific.

The campus is a colorful melting pot of students and an ideal environment for courses in sociology and race relations. An electronic language laboratory simplifies the study of Oriental languages. Those of mixed racial backgrounds are now called Cosmopolitans—a term coined by the University. Once a year when the springtime beauty contest is held, a separate queen is elected to represent each of the seven major racial groups, Polynesian, Caucasian, Japanese, Filipino, Korean, Chinese and Cosmopolitan.

Hawaii's schools teach good English, but boys and girls also know the sounds of languages spoken by over half of the world's population, including Japanese, Chinese, Korean, Hawaiian and pidgin English. There are several Chinese language schools and about forty similar Japanese schools. As one father expressed it, "We have to send our children to a Japanese language school so they can understand their grandmother when she comes to visit us."

About one out of every five children from the first grade through high school attends one of the state's one hundred and twelve private schools.

The Kamehameha Schools founded in 1887 expressly for children of Hawaiian ancestry today provide a modern education for nearly two thousand students and offer one of the best examples of private education in the Islands. Here the traditions and culture of old Hawaii are carried on, together with basic American education on up-to-date subjects, in modern classrooms and laboratories. All of the students are full or part Hawaiian, but the majority also have Caucasian, Portuguese, Chinese, Japanese, Filipino or other ancestral strains.

[14]

Kamehameha School buildings and campus at Kapalama Heights stand on a three-hundred-acre site overlooking Honolulu.

When King Kamehameha V asked the beautiful Hawaiian Princess Bernice Pauahi to succeed him as ruler of Hawaii, she refused. By that time she was the wife of Charles R. Bishop of Glen Falls, New York, and she wished to devote herself to the guidance of young Hawaiian people. As the last direct heir to the first king of Hawaii, Princess Bernice Pauahi Bishop inherited the remainder of Kamehameha's vast lands. On her death her will set aside the extensive holdings in perpetual trust to found and maintain the Kamehameha Schools for the education of young Hawaiian boys and girls. All of the income from the land, the largest private holdings in the state, goes solely toward the maintenance and operation of the schools. The legacy is managed by trustees appointed by the Supreme Court of Hawaii.

Four main objectives based on the will of the princess are woven

[15]

into the educational standards at Kamehameha Schools. First is the nondenominational spiritual and moral development of every student.

Second, students are challenged to develop to the fullest their individual capabilities. For boys there are college preparatory courses and courses in business, machine shop, electric shop, wood carving, welding, agriculture, drafting, printing and book binding. For girls there are college preparatory or business courses, home-making, print shop, book binding, library training and museum workshop.

Third in the list of the princess's objectives is an emphasis on dignity of work. Good work habits and a good attitude toward work are taught through an eleventh grade program which provides on-the-job experience in some office or other work area on the campus, and through short daily job assignments given to every student in the fifth through the twelfth grades.

The fourth objective is an emphasis on leadership and community service. A wide variety of class, club, ROTC, student body and athletic activities gives almost every student the opportunity to direct others in some situation.

The three senior practice cottages at the School for Girls are unique for high schools in the Islands or anywhere. Every girl has the opportunity, before she graduates, to live as part of a family unit in one of the cottages—complete with a baby, for which she has the full responsibility for one week.

There are always more applicants than vacancies at the schools endowed by the farsighted princess who was the last of the royal line of Kamehamehas.

Within a radius of six miles in Honolulu there is a Shinto shrine, a Mormon tabernacle, a Catholic cathedral, a Hawaiian heiau (place of worship); a Confucianist, a Taoist and a Buddhist temple; a Korean church, a Jewish temple and Protestant churches of many denominations. All churches have active study groups

[16]

Honolulu's Honpa Hongwanji Temple is of Burmese design. Its gong, made of a secret alloy, carries tones and overtones for three minutes after being struck.

and are important centers of culture and integration for young people of many different faiths.

Buddhism, a gentle and peaceable religion, is the most widespread of Oriental faiths in the Fiftieth State. There are six major Buddhist sects and a membership of nearly one hundred thousand. Present-day Buddhist temples are not only centers of religion but schools and service societies as well.

The Honpa Hongwanji sect which came to the Islands in 1889

at the request of Japanese sugar cane workers was the first Buddhist mission in Hawaii. Today it has forty-nine temples on the four main islands served by forty-six ministers. The main temple is a stone building of Burmese design topped with three Oriental domes. Delicate scrollwork with gold and filigree decorate the interior. In the spacious garden is a sacred bodhi tree that was brought to Hawaii from Buddhagaya where the Buddha attained enlightenment.

Soto-Zen, the meditation sect which came to Hawaii forty-six years ago, has one of the best known of Buddhist churches. Its new temple near downtown Honolulu is visited daily by people from many parts of the world.

Hawaii's newest Buddhist sect, Kegon, was introduced in 1941 by founder-saint Tatsusho Hirai, who was born in Hawaii. She went as a young girl to Japan where she received her education and was made the first woman bishop of the sect, which is one of the oldest in Japan.

Buddhists in Hawaii all subscribe to the same basic beliefs laid down by Gautama Buddha. Their differences arise from the different emphasis each sect puts on the Buddha's various teachings. Buddha taught that to reach nirvana or salvation one must cease from evil, cultivate the good, purify one's own heart and help others. Buddhism has adapted itself to Island surroundings and to many Christian customs unheard of in the Orient, such as pianos, organs, choirs and Sunday Schools.

Shinto, a worship in which the sun is the chief of many gods, has remained of primary appeal to the older Japanese-born people. In speaking of the lack of young interest in Shinto one priest lamented, "Alas, the young people today want facts—not enchantment."

Confucianism, Buddhism and Taoism have become at bottom a combined Chinese folk religion. A visit to any Chinese temple reveals that reverence for the powers of nature and the social bonds of the family characterizes the religious feelings of the Chinese.

Most of Oahu's one hundred and fifty-three churches of various denominations are Christian. Many have boarding schools and day schools for children. In addition to the state's twenty-seven Catholic parochial schools there are a large number of Protestant schools as well as several church-founded colleges and academies.

Freedom of religion prevails. Many faiths and sects worship side by side in harmony. In the Hawaiian tradition the Fiftieth State has adopted as its official creed the old Kamehameha words, *Ua mau ke ea o ka aina i ka pono—The life of the land is perpetuated in righteousness.*

Everywhere in Hawaii there is a strange contrast between Polynesian languor and New England enterprise. The industrious people of Oriental background who never seem to tire are a far cry from the Hawaiian who prefers singing, laughing and enjoying life. The native Hawaiian cannot stand hour-after-hour routine drudgery. But he can work hard and enduringly at what he really likes to do. Many are employed as instructors in swimming or water sports; others sing and play the guitar in night clubs. Some are teachers, policemen and firemen; others drive buses and taxis. A few still fish or eke out an existence raising poi. Those who can prefer to live "the good life of a free man." But, living for the most part as landless orphans in their own abundant islands, their number continues to decline each year.

Young boys, many of them from Hawaiian families, meet incoming passenger ships and dive for coins as the ship edges slowly into the dock. No one dives for pennies or nickels any more. When dimes or quarters are tossed from the ship's deck several swimmers dive swiftly beneath the surface and quickly return with the money in their mouths.

All around the world people know of the Hawaiian custom of giving garlands of flowers, called leis, as tokens of hospitality

The lei is a symbol of Hawaiian aloha and lei-sellers are an Island institution.

and friendship. The giving of a lei is usually accompanied by a
kiss. Many of the older Hawaiian women earn a living making
and selling flower leis for arriving and departing visitors. Their
business is carried on mostly as a sidewalk enterprise and is the
sole support of many families.

It takes from one hundred to three hundred carnations or two
thousand tiny kika blossoms to make a good lei. An average lei,
about eighteen inches long with up to a hundred tiny orchids in
it, can be bought in Hilo or Honolulu from a street seller for one
dollar.

On Lei Day, May first, the Islands are filled with lei queens
elected from grammar schools, high schools and from the University. Contests are held for the most original lei. In an atmosphere of fragrance and friendliness everyone from the Governor
on down to the youngest street sweeper wears a lei.

The carnation, one of the longest lasting flowers, makes
Hawaii's most popular lei. Fragrant plumiera, a common flower
that blooms much of the year, and small white ginger blossoms
that look like tiny moths make excellent leis. The oldest lei flower
is the delicious-scented yellow ginger. In recent years Vanda hybrid orchids have become widely used because they remain fresh
for four or five days and may be shipped over long distances. For
special occasions small creamy white pikake jasmine blossoms
are selected or, for an unusual lei, Chinese violets are sometimes
chosen because of their strange fragrance.

Throughout the year there are a succession of fetes, festivities,
competitions and commemorations. Everyone including the ka-
punas (grandparents) take part in the ceremonies. On the first
day of the Lunar Year, usually in late January, the thirty thousand people of Chinese ancestry celebrate the new year with the
greeting "Kung hei fat choy"—meaning "Happiness and prosperity." During festivities spectacular fireworks are frequently
shot off to frighten the evil spirits away. The fragrant narcissus
flower presides over the first month of the Chinese New Year

Every weekend through July and August colorfully costumed dancers dance "to the dead" in front of Buddhist temples.

and during the Festival of Narcissus lions, unicorns and huge Chinese dragons dance through the streets.

Wesak Day (flower festival), the birthday of Buddha, is celebrated early in April. It is a sort of Buddhist welcome to spring and the renewed earth. It also commemorates Buddha's teachings of peace, love of man and equality. In Honolulu more than ten thousand people gather for sunrise services on Buddha's birthday.

The Cherry Blossom Festival, also in April, is celebrated with folk dancing, sports and tea ceremonies. There is also a Boys' Day and a Girls' Day. Aloha Week, which lasts a month, is the Islands' largest and most colorful festival. In a reenactment of old Hawaiian customs there is a grueling canoe race between islands and a continuous succession of craft demonstrations, pageants, sports, hulas, parades and native style feasts. The hoolau-leu (street dancing of different nationalities) stops all traffic in Waikiki. After the eighth night on Oahu with its traditional banquets and balls each of the other islands has its own week with its own unique historic pageantry.

Some ancient rites that are seen elsewhere only in the Far East are regular events in Hawaii. All summer, on the lawns in front of their temples, Japanese Buddhists honor the dead with Bon Dances that date back thirteen hundred years. Dance teams in kimonos and straw hats decorated with cherry blossoms dance to the reedy tunes of flutes and to the beat of giant drums. Bon Dances honor the dead with joy instead of sadness because in the Buddhist tradition they have entered paradise.

Late in August Chinese Buddhists gather below Waikiki for ceremonies of the Dragon Boat Day to pacify dieties of the sea so they will bless swimmers and ocean travelers. Food offerings sprinkled with tea and whiskey are placed under the palm trees. Strange boats of brilliant-colored paper representing a dragon breathing fire and a phoenix bearing the Goddess of Mercy are set afloat as gongs ring and a priest reads from a red prayer book.

[23]

The boats are then set afire to send them to the world beyond. Candles are sent afloat in gay decorated containers to light the way of the departed ones.

During Aloha Week or on other special days if a visitor is invited to a Hawaiian hale (home) he goes makai (toward the sea), or if the house is in the direction of the blue-green Koolau range behind Honolulu he goes mauka (toward the mountains). At the Island home he most likely is seated in an open patio or lanai which takes advantage of outdoor beauty and the refreshing trade breezes. Sometimes passion fruit sherbet is served floating in a pineapple or iced tea with a "stick" of pineapple. For dinner he will probably be offered poi (taro root paste), lomi lomi (minced salmon mixed with chopped tomatoes and onions) and barbecued pig, or hot laulau, which consists of cubes of pork, salted fresh butterfish, green onions and Hawaiian spinach (taro leaves) wrapped tightly in ti-leaves and steamed for hours.

At the home of a first-generation Japanese family the visitor removes his shoes as he enters the house. When dinner is served it is on a low table and the guest sits on the floor or on a zabuton (floor cushion). Perhaps the main food is chicken or beef teriyaki. On New Year's day he is served kobu (seaweed), which brings happiness, kuromame (black beans), for health, and kazunoko (fish eggs) for prosperity.

An invitation to a Chinese dinner is printed on red paper, which signifies happiness. If the invitation contains a picture of a bearded old man with a staff, a guest knows it is an invitation to a birthday dinner. Shark fin soup, won ton (the Chinese version of ravioli), bean sprouts and sweet red pork or pineapple spareribs could be the dinner.

In a Filipino home the meal may consist of bitso-bitso (grated sweet potatoes fried in fat), bud bud (rice and coconut in a banana leaf), adobo (a pork dish) or inehaw (broiled fish stuffed with chopped onion and tomatoes). For dessert perhaps maruya —a fried banana done in butter—is served.

[24]

A Hawaiian family enjoying their favorite Island foods, poi and laulau.

On a weekend luau (a Hawaiian pit feast) a whole pig is steamed in the ground, together with many delicacies wrapped in taro leaves. Besides pig, natives serve cool bowls of starchy gray-blue root paste poi, limu (seaweed), chicken cooked with taro in coconut milk, bananas, sweet potatoes, and mullet baked

[25]

in ti-leaves. Almost everyone likes the tangy taste of taro leaves cooked like spinach, the golden ripe pineapples and delicious coconut and arrowroot pudding.

Poi, the native Hawaiian staff of life, is a pinkish-gray glutinous paste made from the starchy root of the taro plant. The root must first be steamed for hours to break down the tiny crystals that would otherwise cut one's tongue. It is then peeled and pounded into a thick paste, allowed to ferment, and finally mixed with water to form a one-finger, two-finger or three-finger thickness.

The first and second fingers are usually used to dip up the poi with a deft twirl followed by a quick circular flourish to prevent drippings. The poi adhering to the fingers is inserted at once into the mouth and the process finished with a polite sucking of the fingers. To eat it neatly requires much practice and to enjoy it takes even longer. Most malihinis (newcomers) dislike the taste very much—some say it tastes like wallpaper paste—but long-time residents acquire a real fondness for the highly nutritious paste.

Early luaus were held in a spirit of thanksgiving to the gods. At a luau everyone sits crosslegged on the ground or floor. All luau food is properly eaten with the fingers, including the pudding, which is served on a ti-leaf and made firm enough to be picked up in small cubes. After eating, everyone shares in the merrymaking.

A variation of the luau is a Hawaiian curry party. One of the best Island curries is made with a sauce of rich coconut milk served with fresh grated coconut and mango chutney. The rice with shrimp, chicken or other meat is topped with layers of macadamia nuts, diced bananas, pickled pineapples, crisp bacon squares, hard cooked eggs, and so forth. A family curry of five layers is called a "five boy curry"—a name borrowed from India where each boy has his own condiment to prepare and serve. A festive dinner is often an eight boy curry but can be a ten, twelve or twenty boy curry.

In place of hats many Islanders wear fresh flowers in their hair. Bright floral-design Aloha shirts are worn by men and colorful muumuus—"Mother Hubbard" gowns—are more popular with women than any other type of dress. The Aloha shirt worn with the shirttail tucked in or left out is acceptable at school and at all parties or informal dinners. The muumuu, which is many things to many people, is worn as a night gown, bathing suit or dinner dress, and has come a long way from the sacklike "down-to-the-toes" garment introduced by the missionaries. Today the muumuu is acceptable for almost any social gathering and comes in bright Polynesian prints, with butterfly and kimono sleeves, with slit sides, low necklines and perky collars.

Many boys and girls go about barefooted, which is considered perfectly proper at home parties and most other places. However, some schools require that young people start wearing shoes and stockings when they enter the seventh grade. In Honolulu's main downtown department store so many bare toes got pinched in the escalator that they now have signs requiring riders to wear shoes.

A picnic for young people more often than not is located in or near the water. To reach it, Islanders have modern three-speed bicycles, motor scooters, hot rods and jalopies; or they drive the family car loaded with friends, just as young people do in San Francisco or Boston. Sometimes large groups go fishing with long nets, which they all pull in together with much laughter and singing. This type of fishing party is called a hikilau and usually ends in a feast. Moonlight or torchlight swimming and diving is popular. During nights when the sea is light and the moon is up, divers wading about in the shallow reefs come across fish that are seldom seen in the daytime. Two of the species most frequently seen by night divers are the white conger eel (considered a deli-

Thirty to forty foot seas thunder in at Makaha, where the world's best surfers compete annually.

cacy) and the "night squid," an octopus that prefers the nocturnal hours. The menpachi, or red fish, also emerge from their coral recesses at night. When the moon disappears and divers have to leave the water, lobsters are observed leaving their holes under cover of darkness.

Riding a surfboard is the most popular and also the most difficult of beach sports, and it takes many years to acquire enough skill to do it well. Experts, usually men with ten years or more of training, can stand on their hands or carry someone on their shoulders while racing along on the foaming crest of a breaker at thirty miles an hour. Those without skill sometimes get badly bruised from the ten-foot, sixty-six-pound surfboard if they lose their balance and fall into a wild tumbling sea. Occasionally someone gets seriously injured and a few have been killed.

There are many things for young people to do besides swimming, water skiing, fishing, boating, beachcombing and shell collecting. All the usual ball games are played. Tennis and horseback riding are popular. Hiking and camping are encouraged on the many trails and on the beaches. Overnight camping is permitted by the State Board of Forestry at some camps.

During the wet season those who want to do something different go ti-leaf sliding. The game consists simply of sitting on a batch of large, tough ti-leaves and sliding down a long, steep mountain slope at breathtaking speed. It is more fun, or as young Islanders say, it is "more pupule" (Hawaiian for crazy) to do it right after a heavy rain because the muddier the slope the swifter and more exciting the ride.

A picnic lunch at the beach will sometimes consist of steak strips soaked overnight in teriyaki sauce and threaded, five or six bite-size pieces at a time, onto thin bamboo skewers and broiled lightly over charcoal. Some prefer to eat the tasty strips raw. Fried won tons, pig toasted on a spit or Japanese hekka are popular at parties. Equally popular is the hula-burger which is a hamburger, a fried egg, a slice of cheese and a slice of tomato served in a bun with pickle and olive. At night parties by flickering torchlight the prime favorite of young Island people of all races is "meat-stick" teriyaki. Some malihinis (newcomers) even learn to like Japanese sashimi (raw fish). Saimen shops—small Japanese restaurants—serve noodle soup and teriyaki-on-a-stick at hamburger prices. Often at a Portuguese bakery there is a line of cars waiting for piping hot malasadas (Portuguese-style doughnuts) and for pao doce (sweet bread made with eggs).

At a beach gathering there is always singing to the soft rhythms of the ukulele, an instrument introduced to Hawaii by early Portuguese cane cutters. A few of the old missionary hymns have been transformed into dreamy melodies and are occasionally sung at night to the light of kukui-nut torches. The latest Island songs and rock 'n' roll music from the Coast are heard more often than not.

A wide variety of instruments are played by young Islanders, including the Korean chung-goo, the Hawaiian eke-eke, Japanese koto, Chinese butterfly harp and others. Though Hawaiian folk music has virtually disappeared, the ukulele and the guitar have the status of folk instruments. Percussion instruments are popular and young Islanders beat out hula rhythms on more than a dozen instruments made of gourds, skins and plants. The calabash gourd, known as the ipu, is slapped by hand to produce a resonant hula rhythm. Dancers frequently use the uluili, a rattling gourd about the size of a small grapefruit, and the puli, an instrument that gives a rustling sound when tapped. The puli is a section of bamboo about eighteen inches long split lengthwise in narrow sections. Island castanets, called lliili, are small water-worn stones held in the palm of a dancer's hand and clicked together rhythmically.

When there is music there is always the hula. Schools teach it in gym classes and most schoolgirls take hula lessons for training in posture and gracefulness. The authentic hula is hard to learn. It is slow, intricate and graceful. At one time there were two hundred and sixty-two different versions.

Hawaiian girls warm up for a puli (bamboo stick) hula in Honolulu's Queen Kapiolani Park.

The real Hawaiian dancers wear only fresh green ti-leaves. Their fluttering fingers portray the ripples of waves, the flight of birds or the falling of rain. A dancer's hips maintain rhythm and the feet keep the time. A rippling of hands and arms means lightning, an upturned hand with fingertips meeting denotes a star, arched fingers signify a rainbow. Any story of nature can be told beautifully by a good hula dancer.

Traditionally Hawaii has always extended hospitality and good will to the people of other nations. Aloha, the spirit of the Islands, means gracious welcome more than anything else. New-comers are called malihinis and upon arrival are made welcome with garlands of fresh flowers. Those who "belong" are referred to as kamaainas. A person can live in the Islands twenty years and never be a true kamaaina, while the right person becomes one very soon. The true kamaainas must have the feel of the land; their hearts must be with the people and the Islands.

A few years ago in Hawaii most of the people worked on pine-apple and sugar plantations. Today with improved methods and the development of modern plantation machinery most people are office workers, farmers and factory and cannery employees. What was once a number of "cultural islands" in Honolulu known as "Chinatown," "Tourist Waikiki," "Hell's Half Acre," "Silk Stocking Manoa" (Manoa Valley Caucasian area) and other distinctly separate areas has been integrated into the over-all community. As in mainland cities, people work for the Army, Navy and Air Force, stores, public utilities and hotels, and many are in small businesses for themselves. People start to work earlier and quit earlier than on the mainland.

The people of the new Fiftieth State are young and vigorous, (ten years younger than the mainland average). They are weary of having the Islands on the one hand thought of solely as an American Gibraltar, and on the other hand sought after by tour-ists as a languorous mecca of grass huts and sleepy-eyed Polyne-sians living on poi and fish. They can remind you that Hawaii had a printing press and the first good schools west of the Rockies when California was still a wilderness. They are able to point out that the people of Hawaii rate high according to any standards in health, sports, culture and education.

Mixed marriages among the seven major races have resulted in more than one hundred and twenty different combinations of races and faces. In Hawaii a visitor sees qualities that are a credit to all the races. He sees people of outstanding character and attractiveness.

Islanders are serious citizens. In an election almost all of the residents turn out to vote. In 1959 two of the first representatives that the Fiftieth State sent to Washington were of Chinese and Japanese extraction. Able and outstanding as they were in the Island legislature, they brought to Congress a type of leadership well grounded in the American principle of equality for all.

Hiram Leong Fong, the first person of Asian descent ever to sit in the United States Senate, is a self-made millionaire whose father worked in the cane fields for twelve dollars a month. Fong, who changed his name from Yau to Hiram, worked his way through high school by selling newspapers and shining shoes. Daniel Ken Inouye, the first U. S. Congressman of Japanese descent, won a battlefield commission and fourteen decorations for heroism with the celebrated 442nd ("Go for Broke") Regiment. In the Po Valley Inouye with a grenade-shattered right arm refused evacuation and directed the final assault that carried the ridge.

Out of the Hawaiian melting pot statehood is bringing a distinctive new Islander to the fore. Many Islanders feel that, with more than half of the world's inhabitants living in Asia, the future peace of the world lies with the people of Oceania.

[33]

Chapter two

HAWAII TODAY: THE ISLANDS

To MANY AMERICANS HAWAII IS SIMPLY A GROUP OF ISLANDS OUT in the Pacific. Few realize how important its geographical location really is. Few know that all the American military and naval forces in the Pacific are under the unified command of one man on Oahu who is responsible for a Pacific area reaching from Alaska to the Asian shores—the largest military command in the history of the world.

A look at the map will show you that the new Island State lies in the mid-Pacific almost halfway between the United States and China. The land, rising steeply out of the sea, is unlike any continental state. You will see that it is at the center of a vast open sea area bordered by four continents. You will realize at once why it is an important crossway of the sea and air and a vital link between the East and the West.

Long before the first man appeared on earth a rift opened in the ocean floor and thrust up great masses of lava to form what is now known as the Fiftieth State. The five major islands of the sixteen hundred mile long Hawaiian Archipelago and its atolls and reefs that extend from the big Island of Hawaii northwestward to Midway and Kure are the tops of the tallest mountains in the world. These volcanic peaks of land are all that is visible of a submerged mountain range which if located on the Pacific Coast would reach from Alaska to Mexico City. So deep is the

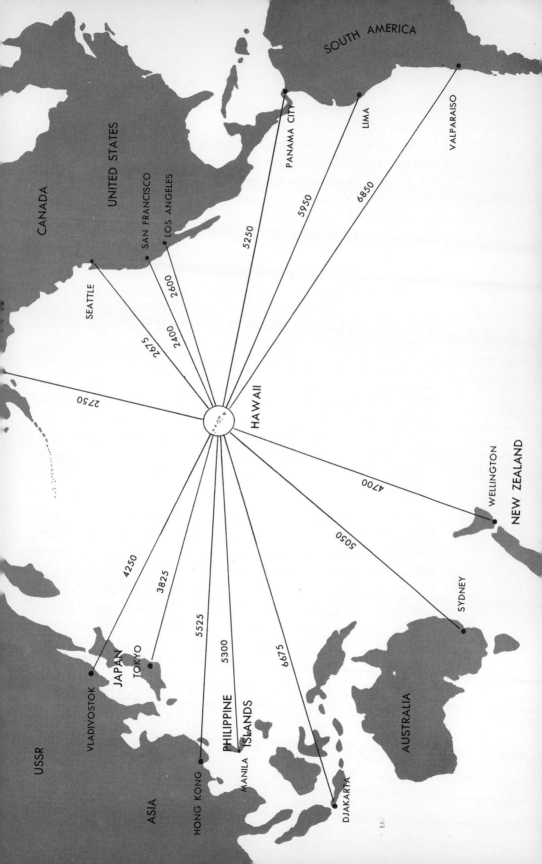

SOUTH AMERICA

CANADA

UNITED STATES

PANAMA CITY

LIMA

VALPARAISO

SAN FRANCISCO

LOS ANGELES

SEATTLE

5250

5950

6850

2600

2400

2675

2750

HAWAII

WELLINGTON

NEW ZEALAND

4700

5050

4250

3825

5525

5300

6675

SYDNEY

VLADIVOSTOK

JAPAN

TOKYO

PHILIPPINE

ISLANDS

MANILA

HONG KONG

ASIA

USSR

AUSTRALIA

DJAKARTA

ocean around the main islands that these peaks must rise eighteen thousand feet just to form dry land.

The cool, refreshing east and northeast winds and the ocean currents that drift down in a great circle from the north keep the Islands cooler than the tropics. The trade winds blow all year round and almost continuously during the summer months, giving the state a climate that local residents describe as "the kind of weather California would like to have." The temperature rarely goes below 72° or above 76°. But the rainfall varies greatly, especially on the high islands where it is extremely heavy on the windward northeastern slopes, and in the mountains where it pours into rushing streams and small rivers that tumble down through fertile valleys to the sea.

When Islanders say Hawaii they mean all of the islands, though Hawaii is the proper name for only the southernmost island of the group. When a traveler in San Francisco says, "I am going to Hawaii," he usually means he is going to Honolulu, which is on the important Island of Oahu one hundred and eighty miles north of the Island of Hawaii. So, let's look at the map again.

Honolulu

Honolulu, the capital, principal port and largest city in the State of Hawaii, is protected from the wind and seas of the windward coast by a rugged mountain range rising steep and green beyond the residential heights. As the hub of the north central Pacific, it has become a world shipping and aviation center only nine hours' flying time by jet plane from New York City. Its air lines and sea lines open out to Japan, China, the Philippines, the Dutch East Indies, Australia, New Zealand and to most of the main islands in between.

Honolulu, like New York City, has a mixture of religions, races customs and cultures that are in the process of becoming thoroughly American. From a tiny village of thatched huts, once a

[36]

haven for windjammers, it has become the fastest-changing modern city in America, with more cars per capita than Chicago or Philadelphia. In the new order of things it is a mecca for tourists and a busy cosmopolitan trade center. It is also a city of broad contrasts. In downtown Honolulu you can sit on the lawn of the only royal palace in the United States. A few blocks away in the financial center you can cash a check from any bank in the world. Within five minutes' walk you can buy an octopus, a pound of soybean cheese, a dried duck or a dozen aged eggs encased in mud.

If you go down to Pier 15, only a few blocks from the business and financial center of the city, at 5:30 A.M., you see huge marlin and tuna being hoisted from the boats to the dock. An hour later the tinkling of a small hand bell starts the daily fish auction. Bids come fast and the auctioneer moves quickly down the line of big fish handing out tags for each to the highest bidder. At another market buckets and tubs of rainbow-colored small fish, mackerel and eels are auctioned. In the retail market you can buy red, pink or stripped snappers, apupu and squirrel fish as well as small sacks of poi, Oriental smoked meats and shellfish. Near the fish market a kamaboko factory turns out Japanese fish cakes.

In Honolulu restaurants are exotic. Many have unique names such as Queens Surf, Tin Tin Char Sut, and Teahouse of the Golden Dragon. At Waikiki you can eat in a tree, sitting high up in the top branches of a spreading banyan at the International Market Place. You can eat American food as well as Hawaiian, Chinese, Japanese, French, Italian, Mexican and Korean. Most colorful are the laulau (pork with salmon wrapped in leaves), sukiyaki and fu yung dinners. You can have Japanese tempura (fish delicately fried in rapeseed oil), pipi kaula (Hawaiian spiced meat), Chinese glazed duck, swallows' nests and sugared pork or Korean kun koki (seasoned broiled meat with pulverized sesame seeds).

[37]

The port of Honolulu, showing central downtown business section, residential areas, Waikiki Beach surf and Diamond Head in the background.

Honolulu, despite its growing pains, is still a flower-lovely city of enchantment and beauty. Royal palms grow from the sea up into the lower slopes of the mountains. There are always billowing clouds and trade winds to rustle the coco palms. There are many miles of ponds with quaint rounded bridges and canals afloat with blue and white water lilies. Along the palm-lined residential avenues, in place of fences, there are often purple bougainvillea, lavender jacaranda and fragrant oleander hedges. In place of porches many houses have broad, vine-covered verandahs, called lanais. Community life in general is the same as you might find in any large California or Florida city.

Over half of the total population of the new state lives in Honolulu, which can expand only on the hundreds of acres of "new land" being dredged up out of the offshore coral reefs. Waikiki's long sweep of white sand is bordered with luxury hotels and the trend is skyward. In 1960 there were sixty-one hotels in the dense beach area and more under construction. Good land, if you can find any in the city, sells for two to three dollars a square foot. Choice land along the heart of Waikiki's "mile of romance" is valued at twenty dollars a square foot. Nearly five thousand acres of the most valuable land in Honolulu has been added to the island by the Walter F. Dillingham technique of filling in shallow water and swampy areas with coral fill. Blocks of new houses are still mushrooming out of the reclaimed swamps and tidelands in an effort to meet the demand for more living space.

Oahu

Oahu, meaning "the gathering place" in Hawaiian, has more than three-quarters of the state's population within its shorelines. Made up of two ranges of mountains with bluff old Diamond Head as its sentinel, it is an island of steep green peaks rising over four thousand feet, with sugar cane plantations and blue-green pineapple fields stretching far over the lower slopes and

Oahu's Hanauma Bay, the remains of one of the ancient craters, is one of Honolulu's favorite picnic beaches.

fertile valleys. Up Nuuanu Valley is the spectacular Pali where sheer cliffs drop to the green windward coastal lands. Over these cliffs Kamehameha I drove the Oahu warriors in his last fierce battle to unite the Islands.

The people who live around the slopes of the island are so close to the mountains and to the sea that they use old Hawaiian words to indicate directions, "mauka" meaning "toward the mountains," and "makai" "toward the sea." On those few days of the year when the trade winds are not blowing slope dwellers can actually choose their own climate. If they are too warm at ocean level they drive mauka (toward the mountains) and in a few minutes will rise one thousand feet or more where the temperature drops four or five degrees.

There are thirty-two public beach parks along the island's coastline. Billboards and advertising signs are strictly forbidden on the modern highways that wind through forests and along plantations and shore lines. Little villages with shady banyan and ironwood trees and palm-clad beaches are scattered along its many miles. On the windward side above quiet little Kahana Bay mango, banana and breadfruit trees extend far up into a picturesque tropical valley. At Waimanalo on the beautiful windward coast much of the island's fruit and vegetables are grown. A few miles south of Waimanalo is the blow hole of Koko Head, a natural phenomenon where the sea rushes up through a hole in the lava and throws geysers high into the air. On the north coast there is Wahiawa, a plantation town and home of the world's largest pineapple plantation.

Sharp differences in altitude, rainfall and soil restrict agriculture on Oahu as on the other islands. Less than eight percent of the state's total land is flat enough to be suitable for growing crops. But a plentiful supply of water plus a perfect climate make it possible to cultivate crops the year round and get the maximum yield from the land.

Oahu is Hawaii to most tourists. Wild ginger leis, outrigger canoes, colorful catamarans (swift sailboats with twin hulls) and surfboarding have done much to glamorize the island's beaches and build the tourist trade into the state's third industry. Surfing is as popular with the haoles (whites) as with the native Hawaiians. It has given Waikiki Beach a unique place among the world's vacation spots.

Actually, the favorite beaches for top-notch body surfers are Makapuu on the windward coast and—in the winter—Makaha, where the waves are huge and break long. Surfing off these beaches in strong seas requires mastery of the art of timing and balance. In January during the International Surfing Championships at Makaha the world's top surfers perform in giant seas thirty-five feet or more in height.

The ox carts and grass huts surrounded by hula girls that many tourists expect to find are no longer a part of island life and have not been for many years. The grass-shack "Hawaiian villages" that visitors "discover" at Waikiki were built and are maintained for the benefit of the hundred-million-dollar-a-year tourist trade. Professional entertainers dance the hula, sing and play all the parts. During the peak tourist season Waikiki is incredibly crowded, as is Honolulu. But Waikiki is only a small section of Oahu and Honolulu is not Hawaii any more than Los Angeles is California.

Seven miles west of Honolulu, Pearl Harbor Naval Base is located on a huge, perfectly landlocked bay that spreads out, like an open hand, over twelve square miles in area. From a small coal dump and poorly constructed Naval Drydock that collapsed into the bay in 1913 Pearl Harbor has developed into the world's greatest naval base. (Natives claimed angry sharks caused the drydock to collapse because it was built over the home of the shark queen's son.)

Profound changes have taken place in Hawaii's defense techniques. Since the disastrous 1941 surprise attack the number of warships within Pearl Harbor is kept at a minimum. Guided missile batteries and Honest John rockets are included in the latest island-based defense weapons. At sea, nuclear submarines and the most advanced supersonic jets have been added to the watchdog patrols of the Pacific Barrier Command.

A few trusts, corporations and individuals hold most of the private land. Ten big estates own twenty-five percent of all the land on Oahu. Much of it is still held in huge slices which reach from the mountains to the sea and date from the Great Mahele (division of land) which took place more than a century ago. Ninety percent of Honolulu's residents do not own any land at all; most of the big estates choose to lease rather than sell their land. Many hundreds of residents own their homes and businesses without owning the land on which they sit. In 1959 the state legislature, looking toward reducing the old feudal landholdings, enacted the first major land reform legislation since Kamehameha III's Great Mahele. The new legislation provided for the purchase or legal condemnation of land by the state and redistribution to Hawaiians who wished to buy homesites.

The Island of Hawaii

One hundred and ninety-four miles southeast of Honolulu, the legendary, looming-blue Island of Hawaii is almost twice as large as all of the principal islands put together. It is shaped somewhat like a triangle and its greatest length is eighty-three miles north and south with an extreme width of seventy-three miles.

Hilo, on the shores of crescent-shaped Hilo Bay, is the new state's second city in size and importance. It is the gateway through which all of the famous Kona coffee and two-thirds of the total sugar grown in the Islands is shipped to Honolulu and the Pacific Coast. In recent years Hilo has become known as the orchid capital of America. More than fifty million orchids a year are sent to the mainland by air freight. The town, beautifully situated along the northwest shores of the bay, combines all of the features of a modern shipping and agricultural center with the warm color and atmosphere of a tropical village.

The Island of Hawaii's snow-capped Mauna Kea, an extinct volcano, is the highest mountain in the Pacific, reaching to 13,784 feet above sea level. Nearby Mauna Loa, famous in Island legends as the home of Pele the fire goddess, is one of the most frequently active volcanoes on earth. Every few years when Mauna Loa erupts, old-timers claim it is attempting to gain the extra one hundred and four feet that will make it as high as Mauna Kea. Mount Kilauea, which is thought to be an outlet for the same lava source that feeds Mauna Loa, has been the more active of the island's two live volcanoes in recent years. The whole area around Kilauea spouts sulphurous steam. Both craters could erupt at any time.

Large areas of the island are covered with lava flows. When Kilauea "blew its lid" in 1955 and 1959, hot lava covered many hundreds of acres of sugar cane, coffee farms and fruit orchards. During Mauna Loa's 1950 eruption molten lava flowed for twenty-three days from a fissure thirteen miles long. At Puna, the scene of Kilauea's last eruption, you smell the sulphur, see the hot cinder cones and feel the rumbling in the quaking ground beneath your feet. Volcano House, a unique hotel on the rim of Kilauea Crater, heats its rooms with volcano steam and you can have steam baths from thick white steam piped direct from volcano vents. Walking along its nearby trails requires stepping around many steam vents.

Molten lava simmers forty-five miles below the surface of the earth and may take years to reach the crater. Unlike the explosive rock and ash of Italy's Vesuvius, Hawaii's fluid lava pours out freely and moves so slowly that it offers little danger. When Kilauea's fire pit is in action fountains of fire from the boiling lava can be seen from the crater rim without danger. Native Hawaiians always used to stay clear of this area for fear of angering Pele and bringing on an eruption.

For a week beginning late in November, 1959, the quarter-mile-wide crater of Kilauea Iki spouted fountains of crimson, molten lava a thousand feet high.

In the rain belt that surrounds the craters the land is a green wilderness where ferns grow twenty feet high, and on the rugged eighty-thousand-acre uplands wild mountain sheep, pigs and goats are found. In the winter the snow-capped peaks provide good skiing for the people from Hilo and surrounding communities.

It is a strange feeling to stand on a clear day in an orange, papaya or breadfruit grove looking up at snow-capped peaks in the distance, knowing that in one hour you can go from a tropical beach up past fern groves and then through freezing temperatures to snow-covered mountains.

In the morning, after the sun raises the temperature of the land, the moisture-laden trade winds sweep in and rise so that by noon the upper slopes of the mountains are usually blanketed in clouds about two thousand feet high. Mistlike showers called "liquid sunshine" are frequent on the windward slopes. But no one pays much attention. Light drizzle-showers are accepted in Hawaii in the way that people along the Pacific Coast accept moisture-laden fog.

The heart of Old Hawaii, and much of its charm, is still to be found on the leeward side of the "Big Island" in little sun-sleepy villages below the coffee farms on the placid Kona Coast. The elder natives living in Kona rarely go to Honolulu and seldom visit Hilo. Most are content to fish, cultivate their gardens, and quietly pass the time in their outrigger canoes and in tiny brown houses that are frequently covered with great masses of fragrant bougainvillea.

Sleepy little Milolii, southernmost village on the Kona Coast, is such a quiet place that it seems like an abandoned settlement. Its hundred native residents make their living fishing from outrigger canoes and sampans.

The waters off Kona's scenic shores are popular fishing grounds for many game fish, including rainbow-colored Mahimahi (dolphin), torpedo-swift wahoos, yellowfins (tuna) and mighty marlin, the king of game fish. All fish species run big. More than thirty world's-record fish have been taken in Hawaiian waters.

In the heart of Kona's coffee plantations, which extend for nearly forty miles, are many little towns. Each town has a coffee mill and usually a single country store that handles everything from strawberry jam to kerosene lanterns. Most coffee farmers have small, six-acre to fifteen-acre family-operated farms. The schools in the area close in the fall at the peak of the coffee harvesting so that the boys and girls can help pick the coffee berries. After the picking, the bright red berries are spread out on roof tops to dry and are then sent to the mill to be graded and bagged for export. Kona coffee is noted for its fine flavor and widely used for blending purposes, especially in Europe, where premium grades are required. It is also used in most American blends.

High lands between the Kona and the Hamakua Coasts are used mostly for ranching and truck gardening. About half of the state's three hundred and eighty-six cattle ranches are located on the Big Island. The three hundred thousand acre Parker Ranch on Waimea Plateau is the second largest Hereford cattle ranch in the world. Its founder, John Parker, was a sailor who married a Hawaiian girl and developed his own domestic herd from the wild cattle he captured in the mountains. Later, imported Hereford entirely replaced the wild Longhorns. Thirty-five thousand head of cattle now roam the Parker Ranch and Hawaiian paniolas (cowboys) ride range on this wide open outpost of the wild west.

Beyond the fertile sugar-cane lands of the Hamakua Coast lies Waipio Valley, one of the most remote and beautiful places in the state. This peaceful valley that was once the home of two thousand people now contains about twenty Chinese-Hawaiians who raise taro and haul it out over the precarious trails on the backs of small mules.

In Hilo and Honolulu you hear it said that in another ten years there will be standing room only on Waikiki Beach. But

[47]

everyone knows that Waipio, with its mile and a half of crescent-shaped beach at the base of towering cliffs, will remain the same. It has hardly changed at all in the past half-century. Sheer cliffs two thousand feet high surround and flank the valley to the edges of the sea. The crude shelflike trails that lead down into the broad lower area, with its crazy-quilt patches of taro, are too steep and dangerous for anyone in a hurry.

Maui

Maui, the "Valley Island" separated from the big Island of Hawaii by a thirty-mile channel, is next to it in size. Shaped somewhat like an ear with a large lobe, it is a double island with high mountains at each end that are joined by a great fertile plain of sugar and pineapple plantations.

Wailuku, the third largest town in the state, is located on Maui's northern coast at the mouth of beautiful Iao Valley. The site of the first crude sugar mill set up on the island, today it is surrounded on all sides by the great cane fields that cover the slopes of the West Maui mountains. The coastal drive from Wailuku to Lahaina is often alive at night with the lights of islanders out torch fishing.

Lahaina, twenty-two miles across the island from Wailuku, was formerly the royal capital of the Kamehameha Kings. Backed by towering blue mountain peaks and sheltered by thick groves of coconut palms, it extends for two miles along the placid leeward shore. During the whaling era, when large numbers of whale ships anchored in the Lahaina Roadstead, the town rivaled Honolulu in importance. Its high school, opened in 1831 and the oldest west of the Rockies, maintains an outstanding program in vocational and agricultural training. In 1834 the *Lama Hawaii,* first newspaper to be published in the Pacific area, was printed here.

Maui's terrain varies from barren mountains to rain-clouded

[48]

peaks, to green valleys and low cattle ranch grasslands. Its volcanic areas and semi-arid wastelands are in sharp contrast to its well-watered plains. The fertile lower slopes of Mount Haleakala produce much of the island's sugar and are covered with plantations and country homes.

A few small native fishing settlements are scattered along the coasts. The roads are flanked with guava trees and with the broad leaves of hala (pandanus) from which mats and baskets are woven. There are bamboo forests, giant ferns and jungles of the ape plant which has leaves so large they are sometimes used as umbrellas. Some of the spirit of old Hawaii remains in a few villages, Kahakuloa, Wailua and Keanae, for example. Most of the inhabitants raise pigs and taro, weave lauhala mats and baskets from narrow, dried strips of hala tree fronds and go net and spear fishing for a living.

Ten-thousand-foot Mount Haleakala, which dominates half of the island, is the largest dormant volcano in the world. Its giant crater, called the "House of the Sun," is twenty miles in circumference. Along its horseback and foot trails you get a peculiar other-planet feeling from the purplish, orange, red, gray and many-hued cones and bold, twisted lava formations. It is also the home of the silversword, a strange flowering plant unknown anywhere else. A young silversword is shaped like a large ball with hundreds of silvery spikes emerging from a central cluster. A tall stem grows from the center which, toward the end of its life, bursts into vivid purple and yellow blossoms.

On the forty-one mile trip up to the crater of Haleakala from Wailuku there is usually a lei of clouds and frequently dense fog to penetrate. The temperature drops from 75° at Wailuku to freezing and sometimes there are snow flurries at the crater. But if it is your lucky day and the sun is low you will see the Specter of Brocken, which means that you will see your own shadow on a cloud below you, encircled by a rainbow.

[49]

A chain of cinder cones three hundred to a thousand feet high reach across the huge crater of Haleakala.

Lanai

Eight miles off the west end of Maui, eleven-by-eighteen-mile Lanai, called the "Pineapple Island," consists almost entirely of the slopes, valleys and peaks of a single large mountain that reaches 3,480 feet above sea level.

Once maintained as a cattle ranch, the rocky, desolate island was bought in 1921 by James Dole, who began one of the most concentrated large-scale plantation projects in the Pacific. A harbor was blasted in the iron-bound coastline, the land was cleared, paved roads were built, and an island-wide irrigation system was set up. In a few years' time twenty-one thousand acres of pineapples were under cultivation. Today in the harbor below Lanai City cranes load as many as one million, four hundred thousand pineapples into barges in a single busy day.

Molokai

Molokai, located a few miles northwest of Maui and a few minutes by plane from the bustling boomland of Honolulu, is an island that keeps many of the old ways and has more pure Hawaiians than any other major island.

A long, narrow island thirty-four miles long by seven miles wide, it is shaped like an old Dutch shoe. Its rugged north coast is extremely steep and in many cases almost perpendicular, with precipitous gorges and sheer cliffs dropping straight to the sea. In the east, Mount Kamakou rises to a height of 4,970 feet. On the lower southern and western slopes the land rolls gently down, providing a large agricultural region almost entirely given over to pineapple cultivation.

A large part of the agricultural lands on the lee slopes of Molokai are owned by Hawaiian homesteaders and cultivated on shares by the big pineapple companies. Near the center of

[51]

the southern coast, the town of Kaunakakai, with its small harbor and wharf, is the principal shipping point from which cattle, honey and pineapples are sent to Honolulu.

At the eastern tip of Molokai a winding road drops down into peaceful, bowl-shaped Halawa Valley. A few of the people who live there today go out to work on island ranches but most of the inhabitants live off the land and the sea. Many islanders left the valley after the last tidal wave destroyed most of the village that formerly looked out on the sea. The homes are now farther up the valley among the lush foliage, within sight and sound of the waterfalls.

The Hansen's disease (formerly called leprosy) settlement of Kalaupapa is completely isolated from the outside world and from the rest of the island by rugged, two-thousand-foot cliffs and the sea. It is located on the north side of Molokai on a beautiful triangular peninsula. Formerly this was a forbidden area but since sulfone drugs have brought the once-fatal disease under full control anyone can go there to visit. Kalaupapa is now a happy settlement much like any other island community. Many who are cured prefer to remain beneath the towering green cliffs and to know the windswept little peninsula as their home.

Adjoining Kalaupapa Valley, but separated from the settlement by gaunt seaward peaks, are several remote, uninhabited and almost unaccessible valleys on the lofty windward coast. Two of them, Wailau and Pelekunu, are every bit as wild and steeped in beauty as Melville's famous Typee Valley in the Marquesas. Directly facing the rain-bearing northeast trades, both have a profusion of vegetation and long thin waterfalls that cascade hundreds of feet into lower streams. There are wild bananas, guavas and delicious little mountain apples; also abandoned taro fields, breadfruit, pineapples, wild oranges and many wild goats, wild pigs and deer. Entirely cut off from Kaunakakai and the small villages of the southern coast by an almost impassable mountain range, both valleys remain almost the same as they were a hundred years ago.

Kauai

Many people who do not like to be crowded live on the cool green Island of Kauai, ninety-five miles northwest of Honolulu. Called the "Garden Island," Kauai is a round island thirty-two miles in width, and a vastly different island from Oahu. Its pace is leisurely. Its coves and beaches are still unspoiled. If you see someone rushing about you can be almost certain he is a malihini (newcomer) from the mainland.

The interior of Kauai is dominated by 5,075-foot Mount Waialeale, considered one of the wettest spots on earth. Thunderhead clouds bring rain almost day and night on the extreme upper slopes, averaging four hundred and seventy-one inches per year. From the central mass of the Waialeale mountains, located almost directly in the center of the island, great ridges and valleys radiate out in many directions and numerous streams and several rivers contribute an abundant supply of water to the rich agricultural areas. Its Wailua, Hanalei and Waimea rivers are among the largest in the state.

Beginning at lovely Hanalei, almost the entire north, east, south and southwestern coastal regions are given over to fertile plantations that extend back many miles from the sea. All of the sugar and pineapples produced in these areas are shipped from Port Allen at Hanapepe Bay on the south coast, and from Ahukini and Nawiliwili Bay on the southeast coast. Other commercial products include rice, coconuts, macadamia nuts, taro and fruit that is processed into mango chutney, guava jelly, papaya jam and coconut candy. Lihue, the principal town, is located two miles inland from Nawiliwili.

Kauai is the least known and least visited of the large islands

A short distance up the Wailua River on Kauai, giant maidenhair ferns hang from the rocky edges of Fern Grotto.

and is, in many ways, the most beautiful and unspoiled of all. There are a number of picturesque little villages bordering the sea and many wide beaches that possess a far greater degree of natural beauty than famed Waikiki. One of the best is located on the north coast where the verdant greens of Hanalei Valley come down to the sea in a sweeping crescent.

Broad, light green fields of rice alongside dark green patches of taro reach out over the swampy flat lands. Lotus root, used in the making of relish and choice chop suey, is also raised. It was here that the ancient Hawaiians gathered for their gay hulas and athletic contests. The lower peaks and ridges of the Waialeale are all about, and when it rains heavily more than a score of cascading waterfalls are visible from almost anywhere in the valley. Whoever has seen a rainbow in Hanalei, the valley that is called the Birthplace of Rainbows, never forgets the experience.

To the west of lovely Hanalei, along the wild and little-known Na Pali Coast, are thirty miles of ragged cliffs and gorges, a truly gaunt region of silent valleys inaccessible by land either from above or below. Ancient walls of gray, yellow and purple rock fall two thousand feet straight into the sea without leaving a single foot of beach or ledge along the water's edge. Although the early Hawaiians lived in one of the valleys, few haoles (whites) have ever explored beyond Kalalau, because the only approach is from the sea and it is extremely hazardous even in the calmest weather. Uninhabited Na Pali remains an unspoiled world for razorback hogs, wild goats and an occasional adventurer.

One of the island's most spectacular features is the great fissure-formed gorge of Waimea in the southwest region. Worn by millions of years of rains and winds, the gorge reaches over twenty-five square miles and is a mile wide. Its mighty walls of aging rock that rise to over three thousand feet begin the day with cool blues and misty greens that deepen with the afternoon sun to gold, copper and flaming reds. Although Waimea is considerably smaller than the Grand Canyon of the Colorado, its similarity in form and coloring has made it widely known as the Grand Canyon of Hawaii.

Niihau

The Forbidden Island of Niihau, lowest and next to the smallest of the main islands, lies twenty-two miles off the west coast of Kauai. Extending sixteen miles in a northeasterly direction and averaging from three to five miles in width, the island is scored on the windward side by deep valleys, rises in the west to a 1,281-foot mountain mass, and slopes gradually away to the shore on the leeward side.

The Forbidden Island is now held by the Robinson family, the descendants of early Scotch settlers who originally purchased it for about twenty-two cents an acre and have ruled its native inhabitants as a private community for nearly a hundred years. In their earnest desire to keep the full-blooded Hawaiians pure and their morals unaffected by whites, the owners, who control the means of transportation, strictly forbid outsiders' visiting Niihau and the native inhabitants' visiting other islands except on the rarest occasions. Anyone wishing to leave the island can do so, but unless permission has been given, he cannot return. School, church and most community affairs are conducted in the Hawaiian language, and although English is taught in the school only a few Islanders are able to speak it well. No radios, telephones, television sets, movies, liquor, tobacco or automobiles are allowed on the island. There is no general store and no need for police or a jail. Homing pigeons are used to send messages to the manager's home on Kauai.

In 1959 there were two hundred and forty-three Islanders living on Niihau, most of whom were pure Hawaiians together with a few hapa-haoles (half-whites). The latter take care of honey production and manage a turkey farm, a fishing enterprise and a

Net casting for fish is just one of many ways in which Hawaiians take food from the ocean.

large pure-bred cattle and sheep ranch. The natives are highly skilled in the weaving of fine makaloa reed mats and in the making of pheasant and peacock feather leis that sometimes sell for as high as fifty to a hundred dollars each in Honolulu. Recently, commercial fishing and the production of charcoal have been added to the Islanders' activities.

Mrs. Elizabeth Sinclair, the Scotch widow of a sea captain and the original pioneer of Niihau, arrived in her own full-rigged ship *Betsy* from New Zealand nearly a century ago, with her children,

[57]

grandchildren, prized cattle, sheep and a huge piano. Mrs. Sinclair bought Niihau and large Kauai holdings outright from King Kamehameha IV for a teakwood box filled with ten thousand dollars in gold coins. Starting with stock ranching the "Family," as the Sinclairs and Robinsons have always been known, expanded and became one of the dominant forces on Kauai.

When the Robinsons are visiting Niihau they go to church in a surrey drawn by Arabian thoroughbreds. In their management of the island they use authority with restraint and are known to give suggestions rather than orders. Working conditions are considered good and the native Hawaiians are apparently quite happy. Of their own accord they keep a strict Sabbath. No riding, hunting, fishing or swimming is done on Sunday. Social life centers about the church and each morning everyone in the family starts the day with prayers and singing.

At the outbreak of World War II, tiny Niihau became the first American soil to be occupied by the Japanese and was the first to be delivered of them. Black smoke was still billowing above the bomb-twisted wreckage of Pearl Harbor when a small fighter plane, bearing the red circle of the rising sun, coughed to a forced landing on Niihau. Dismounting a machine gun from the disabled plane, the pilot, with the help of a local Japanese beekeeper, terrorized the island. When the invader threatened Ben Kanahele, a Niihauan who had killed wild boars with his bare hands, Ben "began to get mad."

"Put that gun down," said Kanahele moving forward.

The aviator shot three times and hit Kanahele in the stomach, groin and leg.

"Then I got mad," Kanahele said later.

The Niihau islander, who was accustomed to carrying two hundred and sixty pound boxes of honey down cliffs to the sea, grabbed the struggling aviator by the leg and quickly smashed him to death against a stone wall.

[58]

When news of the "Battle of Niihau" reached the outside, admiring people acclaimed the event and agreed that despite the piety and peaceful ways of the Niihauans their courage and fighting blood was still something to be reckoned with. For many months people on the big islands chided each other, "Never shoot a Hawaiian three times. He will get mad at you!"

Despite the benevolent policy of the Robinson family there has been criticism of having Hawaiians "quarantined-for-their-own-good." In 1947 a Hawaiian Territorial Senate committee proposed that the territorial government acquire sufficient land, by condemnation if necessary, to open up Niihau to modern "necessities of the twentieth century." Nothing has ever come of the Senate committee's proposal.

Birds and Animals

Changing land uses had all but destroyed Hawaii's wild bird life on the capital island by 1930. Most native birds that remained alive had gone into the mountain forests. Only the raucous, saucy mynahs, the sparrows and gray doves remained. The Honolulu Zoo, which houses one of the world's greatest collections of birds, began actively working with Oahu's Avian Society Hui Manu, the Hawaiian Audubon Society and other groups to conserve and increase the number of wild birds in the islands. Hui Manu has been especially successful in bringing back the gay-colored song birds to the parks and residential areas.

A Junior Hui Manu organization which has been operating for more than a decade has accomplished much toward lowering the number of birds killed by BB guns, air rifles and slingshots. Senior Hui Manu members in school classrooms talk about birds and convince young students that it is far more enjoyable to see beautiful birds in flight and to listen to their songs than it is to destroy their nests and kill them for target practice.

Unknown to most people, jumping kangaroos roam wild and are increasing in numbers in the high forests a short distance from downtown Honolulu. The scarlet iiwi birds that supplied the feathers for King Kamehameha's cloaks are also there. Wild goats share the steeper slopes with wild axis deer that were originally brought to the Islands from India. The axis deer, considered by many to be the most beautiful deer in the world, are the only deer that retain their white spots throughout life. The kangaroo population, descendants of three imported ones that escaped from a private zoo long ago, are known in Australia as the brush-tailed rock wallaby.

The mongoose, another animal from India, has become well established on most of the islands. It was brought into the Islands to take care of the rat problem in the sugar fields but hasn't worked out very well because the mongoose is most active during the day when the rats are asleep, and at night when the mongoose prefers to rest the rats are most active. The traditional diet of the mongoose in its homeland is reptiles, but in Hawaii it must live on rodents, birds and fruits because there are no snakes of any type to be found. Circus snakes and snakes on ships passing through are placed under special guard so that they cannot escape.

Hawaii's large and increasing number of city birds, as well as its unique red, green and yellow forest birds, are now protected by wise laws that prohibit the destruction of many forms of wild life. Even the Hawaiian seals are increasing in number as a result of these protective laws. Once nearly extinct, the Islands' seals are large animals, sometimes seven feet long and weighing over five hundred pounds.

The honey creepers, a family of several dozen species of birds found in abundance in Hawaii, are known for their brilliant colors and strange bills. Some have short, thick bills for cracking seeds; some have medium, pointed bills for feeding on insects; still others have long slender bills for drinking honey nectar from flowers. Honey-creepers were highly prized by the kings of Hawaii for making feather robes, helmets and long capes. The best known honey-creepers are the scarlet apane and the brilliant orange-red iiwi. The California linnet family and the Chinese thrush are also prominent.

The Hawaiian wren, a small, friendly forest bird that has little fear of humans, the island goose and a rare Hawaiian crow that lives on the Big Island are found nowhere else in the world. The rare Hawaiian goose, called the nene, is the official bird of the Fiftieth State. Once nearly extinct, the nene now number about one hundred and fifty and are slowly increasing in a bird reservation on the Kona Coast. The Hawaiian hawk, another bird

The nene, a curious wild goose, is the world's rarest waterfowl. Although a shy bird, it will fight to the death to defend its goslings.

The mysterious night-blooming cereus (left) and one of the many varieties of hibiscus (right) found in the Islands.

that lives only on the island of Hawaii, is called by Islanders the "io," which means the highest point in the sky.

Hawaii's migratory birds, among them the pintail and shoveler ducks and the Pacific golden plovers, fly the longest overwater migrations in the world. These birds are guided by the sun and stars each year as they fly over thousands of miles of open sea from Alaska to Hawaii and back. Long before man learned how to do so, scientists point out, migratory birds were flying vast distances guided by the sun and stars.

The brown, black and white mynah bird from India is easily the most conspicuous bird in the Island State. It is also the least liked among late sleepers because of its loud, sassy screaming in the early mornings. The raucous mynah is always involved in family arguments or making a loud ruckus about something or other, and Waikiki's exclusive hotels consider it almost a major problem. On the other hand, perhaps the most loved birds are the little Japanese hill robins whose beautiful songs can be heard almost any time of the day in the green valleys between the outskirts of Honolulu and the Koolau mountains.

HAWAII TODAY: THE ISLANDS

Flowers and Trees

Bird life in Hawaii would not have such a gay time of it if the Islands did not abound in flowering trees and a general profusion of many of the world's most colorful flowers. But it was not always this way. Early photographs show that most of Honolulu and much of the other islands were once bare and brown. In back of Waikiki's reefs and shorelines were reedy marshes. A single grove of coconut palms were the only trees on a vast sweep as far as a person could see toward Diamond Head. On all of the main islands, large coastal areas were nothing more than dry, bare, dusty plains and foothills reaching from the sea to the mountains without a tree.

Today there are few islands anywhere that are as heavily planted as the Island State. In many sections it is like a botanical wonderland with trees and plants from all over the world. Many have been hybridized and others have taken on characteristics peculiar to their life in Hawaii. As the director of the Botanical Gardens has pointed out, the flowers, like many of the people, can be called Cosmopolitans. The electric light and telephone linemen who have to keep trimming leafy vines and limbs from their poles and wires think that some areas of the Islands are overplanted.

The rare silversword (left), found only in the crater of Haleakala; and the torch ginger (right) which is called the "queen" of Hawaii's many ginger plants.

The one tree that has done more than any other to make the face of Hawaii green and to stop erosion is the kiawe or algarroba, which came to Hawaii from Chile. Great stretches of once-barren areas are now covered with light green forests of kiawe, thanks in part to the boys and girls who were encouraged to distribute the seeds on the driest stretches. In recent years the Honolulu Shade Tree Council was formed to enlarge the number of beautiful trees in the capital city.

A blooming shower tree is a spectacular sight, even if you see it often. Honolulu has shower trees of many colors ranging from a cream-yellow through golden to apricot pink, and there is a yellow and pink variety called the rainbow shower tree. Besides the brilliant red-flowering Poinciana trees from Madagascar one sees startling masses of bougainvillea from Brazil and the vibrant golden yellow flowers of the gold tree. At least one plumiera, or frangipani tree, is found in almost every large garden. These range in color from pure white to yellow and from various shades of pink to a deep maroon red.

The orchid and the hibiscus are probably the two loveliest flowers in the state. Just as the hibiscus is the official flower of the Fiftieth State, the orchid is considered the unofficial "people's flower." There are orchids in nearly every garden and entire front yards are landscaped with them. In the poorest slum districts bonsai trees sit on weatherbeaten porches and orchids are to be seen hanging from rickety landings and balconies. They are seen in the lowest income public housing areas.

The hibiscus, of all flowers, is most typically Hawaiian. From the lovely fragrance of the simple white hibiscus to the spectacular yellows, reds and multi-colors in singles, doubles and splashed forms there are five thousand different hybrid types.

The spectacular, bright orange and blue bird-of-paradise flower and its blue and white blossoming cousin, Strelitzia juncea, grow easily and are seen in the simplest gardens beside anthuriums, orchids and fragrant, waxy gingers.

[64]

Hawaii has special days for flowers like Holland's Tulip Days and Japan's Cherry Blossom Festival, but while flower days in those countries are special events, flowers in Hawaii are a part of everyday living for everybody.

Lei selling, like flower growing, is often a family affair. The standard equipment for a blossom merchant is a small truck or station wagon which parks by special permission in parking areas reserved for lei stands. A table and chairs are set out on the sidewalk with a huge umbrella to protect the flowers from the rays of the sun. Blossoms are withdrawn from a refrigerator compartment inside the car as needed and the leis are strung hourly to the songs and chatter of the lei seller's children.

Flower growers bring their fragrant blossoms each day to the lei stands, which are usually open for business from 9:00 A.M. to 11:00 P.M. If the leis that are strung at night by kerosene lanterns are not sold by closing time they are kept cool and sold the next morning at bargain prices. A fair day's business averages about thirty dollars, and on a boat day when a big liner is in perhaps twice that amount will be taken in by the lei stand owner who is usually part-Hawaiian.

Chapter three

THE FIRST HAWAIIANS

$\mathcal{M}$UCH OF THE CHARM OF THE ISLAND STATE IS AN INHERITANCE
from the early Polynesians. Polynesians have always been by nature a people inclined to welcome other races with a warm spirit of
aloha. No matter where he meets them a person can't help liking
the native Hawaiians. To understand the natural friendliness, the
simple grace and quiet dignity of the Hawaiian people as they are
today we must know something of their background.

When the Hawaiian race was in its ascendancy it displayed
something of Homeric greatness. More than two hundred years
before Columbus and his mutinous crew groped their way across
the Atlantic, at a time when European navigators hugged the
mainland and lived in dread of the sea, bold Polynesians were
making epic voyages unexcelled in the history of any race.

Those first Hawaiians were greater navigators than the Norsemen, and a nobler race. They were a people who cared enough for
beauty to transport flowers over thousands of miles of long-rolling
seas in Stone-Age sailing canoes.

Many perished in the vast void of the world's mightiest ocean.
But they had great faith. They had little fear. They remained at
sea for months at a time with only a simple knowledge of the sea
and the sky. Their huge lateen sails enabled them to sail swiftly,
closer to the wind than any of the European square-riggers that
were to enter the Pacific centuries later.

Native history, told and retold for centuries by word of mouth, reveals that a Polynesian chief sailed over the "rolling water roads" thousands of miles north to Hawaii long before the Norsemen discovered America. Early native legends say that the first people to cross the long rolling "Ocean of Kane" and settle on the Island of Hawaii were led by the great Chief Hawaii-loa, who named the island after himself.

These first Stone-Age settlers, called the Menehune people, are believed to have come from Southeast Asia eastward to the Philippines and on through the low, far-flung islands of Micronesia. Finding few native food plants and no animals on the big, fire-born island, they lived along the coast, constructed many large stone fish ponds, and depended largely on seafoods, berries, roots, and the fruit of the pandanus. Of much smaller stature than the later Polynesians, the Menehune people became known in Hawaiian folklore as the little people.

In the early part of the twelfth century a large influx of new settlers arrived from Tahiti. This second group, a proud, freeborn branch of the Caucasian race, brought their own food plants, animals, flowers and the paper mulberry tree. They subjugated and absorbed the Menehune people and established a more advanced culture. The main islands were divided among their great chiefs and navigators—men such as Hika-po-loa, who remained in Hawaii; Hua and Kalana'-nu'u, who settled on Maui; Newa-lani and Maweke, who chose Oahu; and Puna-nui, who took his people to Kauai. These people from Tahiti, who became known as Hawaiians, were of the Arii—the noblest of Polynesians.

During the period of the first great Crusades in Europe and up until the middle of the thirteenth century, Hawaiian "Vikings" were sailing south to Samoa, Tahiti, Fiji and to other distant lands in quest of adventure and booty. Many of their canoes—black-hulled and sometimes trimmed with red—were from eighty to a hundred feet in length. Built with stone axes and shell tools out of kao wood, they were rigged with coconut fibre sennet, powered

[67]

with matted pandanus sails, and steered by a large stern paddle. On sailing day they were heavily loaded with green coconuts, baskets of dried fish, bamboos filled with fresh water, dogs, fowl and the ever-present bailers. Some carried live pigs for their keen ability to smell land many miles away.

On the long voyage from Hawaii to Tahiti the great canoes took their departure from a channel off Kahoolawe that was named Ke Ala-i-Kahiki, the way to Tahiti. Once out of sight of Kahoolawe, the navigators set a course a little to the east of south, guided, during the first part of the voyage, by Polaris, the North Star, which was kept directly astern. During the day they navigated by the sun, and at night by the thirteen "canoe-steerer's stars." In stormy weather, when the heavenly bodies were obscured, the wind was kept on the port side, as it was known that it was generally easterly.

Polynesian navigators knew how to read the clouds and foretell the presence of land long before it came into view. They knew the phases of the moon. They knew the secrets, the changing positions throughout the year, of more than one hundred and fifty stars. When there were no stars at night and no sun by day they were guided by their knowledge of currents and waves and sometimes by the great flights of migratory birds.

Each year, following an age-old instinct, the Pacific golden plovers and their month-old fledglings arrive in Hawaii non-stop from Alaska. Since the plovers cannot alight on water they must make the twenty-four-hundred-mile flight across the Pacific in forty to sixty hours of steady flying.

The first Hawaiians still had the knowledge that is almost instinctive in those who spend their lives close to the sea and the sky. They had developed a keen sensitivity to air, atmospheric changes and natural lore and knew them almost in the way that birds and sea animals know those things.

Many of the long voyages that were made during this era were celebrated and handed down through songs and genealogies. Together they form a record of skill and seamanship unexcelled by any people. Even more remarkable was their adjustment to the use of weapons, dwellings and agriculture to develop a way of life far in advance of other Pacific islanders.

The early Hawaiians were a handsome, vigorous, well-formed people. Their chiefs were frequently seven feet tall, weighed from three hundred to four hundred pounds and were as accomplished in physical prowess as the best athletes of ancient Greece. They were expert fishermen and craftsmen, and clever warriors. For many centuries they were divided into a number of independent kingdoms that were frequently at war with each other, but their wars were relatively mild affairs compared with the "civilized" European warfare and religious cruelties of that day.

Fish and poi were the main foods. They also had pigs, chickens, bananas, yams, coconuts, breadfruit and sugar cane. The fibrous stalks of the sugar cane were also used for cleaning teeth. Since there was no clay or other suitable material for cooking pots, all the cooking was done in the ground in pit ovens called imus. Enough food was cooked at one time to last for several days.

Men pounded the taro root for poi, fished, built houses, and cultivated sweet potatoes and taro patches. Women made tapa cloth for clothing from the inner bark of the mulberry and wove lauhala mats, pillows, baskets and sails.

Skilled craftsmen cut down great trees with stone adzes. They hollowed tree trunks for sea canoes, and with bone, shell and stone tools made outriggers and carved beautiful paddles. Their calabashes, wooden platters, and other articles of daily use were decorated in bold, plain figures.

Young boys were trained in the fine art of canoe building. Others became skilled in the use of medicinal herbs. Some became historical orators and were specially trained to memorize and recite long traditional songs and chants. Some of the long narratives took a week of evenings or more to tell.

Noblest of primitives, the ancient Hawaiians ranked beauty

[69]

*The old ways are not forgotten. Young Hawaiians still honor the way of life
long ago.*

and grace among the highest of life's gifts. With a perfect climate, excellent health and a plentiful supply of food to be had easily enough, they were able to arrange their ways so as to have a well-planned but minimum amount of work and a maximum of time for sports and for enjoying life.

Mythology formed the most important part of early Hawaiian society and island chiefs, believed by the people to be direct descendants of the gods of Polynesian mythology, were looked upon virtually as earthly gods.

On a stormy night in 1736, during the time of the moon Ikuwa, a child was born in the tiny village of Kokoiki who was destined to become King Kamehameha the First, the greatest figure in Hawaiian history. Coming to manhood during a troubled era, young Kamehameha soon distinguished himself as a great warrior and as the leader of an army of slingers and spear men. By the closing years of the eighteenth century he had become king of the Island of Hawaii with a navy of over eight hundred great war canoes and a following of sixteen thousand well-trained warriors.

An ambitious ruler, Kamehameha devoted much time and thought to the developing of a large fleet of seagoing double canoes with which he intended to transport an army of warriors to the Society Islands to conquer the people of Tahiti. To gain greater size and carrying capacity, huge triple canoes were built combining three hulls into one vessel. But this proved too unwieldy and the idea was eventually discarded. Invading and conquering the Islands of Maui, Molokai and Oahu, and obtaining control over Kauai and Niihau, by 1810 Kamehameha had put an end to the warfare of the rival chiefs, and united the Hawaiian Islands under a single kingdom. In later years he became known as the Napoleon of the Pacific.

Kamehameha used his powers wisely and well. He became as able in preserving peace as he previously was in pursuing war. He protected the common man, kept the best of the old ways and

[71]

curbed the tyranny of lesser chiefs. One of his earliest edicts, issued in the form of a proclamation, has been translated: *Citizens, respect your gods. Respect the big man and the little man. Let the old men, the women and children, walk upon the highway and lie down in the road in peace. Let none disturb them. The penalty is death.*

When peace and security were well established Kamehameha turned to the promotion of agriculture and commerce. He urged all the people, chiefs as well as commoners, to raise food, and took the lead by working with his own hands. "Kamehameha is a good king," observed a native historian. "He builds his own canoe, catches his own fish and tends his own taro patch."

It was during the reign of Kamehameha the First that Hawaii turned from the Stone to the Iron Age, from primitive bone, shell, stone and wooden implements to iron nails, chisels, guns and knives.

The First White Men

The Hawaiian Islands remained unknown to Europeans until after the middle of the eighteenth century. All of the earliest Spanish, Dutch and British voyages from east to west across the Pacific, and the later route of the Manila Galleons from Mexico to the Philippines, passed south of the Hawaiian Islands. The galleons took this course because the winds were favorable and because it avoided the dangerous low-lying Marshall and Caroline Atolls. On the return voyage from Manila to Acapulco, the galleons sailed far to the north of Hawaii in order to take advantage of the strong winds that blow from the west along the thirty-fifth degree of north latitude. Hence, during their lonely voyages across the Pacific, they missed the Hawaiian Islands both coming and going for a period of over two hundred and fifty years, without knowing it.

Hawaiian chief and his paddlers, with protective masks and helmets, hurrying out to Captain Cook's ships.

In December 1777 Captain James Cook sailed from the Society Islands northward along what must have been one of the early routes taken by the Polynesian navigators centuries before. From Christmas Island, which they discovered on Christmas Day, the *Resolution* and the *Discovery* stood again to the north. At daybreak, on the eighteenth of January, 1778, Cook's log reveals that his ships were plunging heavily and making but poor headway against the strong northeast trades when "a high island made its appearance and soon we saw more land entirely detached from the former. On the 19th the island first seen bore east several leagues distant. This being to windward which prevented our getting near it I stood for the other, and not long after discovered a third island."

Both vessels were soon surrounded by hundreds of native canoes as they stood slowly in to anchor off the island of Kauai.

[73]

"What is this great thing with branches?" shouted one chief staring up at the tall masts, spars and rigging of the flagship *Resolution*.

"It is a forest that has slid into the sea," said a second chief.

"It is a floating island," said another.

"It is a great sea canoe!"

"This is no ordinary thing," exclaimed Kuohu, a high priest, holding up his hand for attention. "It is a temple of Lono." He pointed to the ratlines (rope ladders) extending up the shrouds to the tops of the masts. "See the ladders going up to his altars in the clear sky."

"O Lono! Lono," shouted the Hawaiians. "The bones live! Lono has come home."

On boarding the ships the natives plucked at the clothes of the strange white creatures and sniffed their skin. They were especially puzzled by the "fire coming from their faces" (pipes) and "holes in their sides" (pockets).

"In the course of my several voyages," Captain Cook reports, "I never before met with the natives of any place so much astonished as these people were upon entering a ship. Their eyes were continually flying from object to object—and strangely marking to us that till now they had never been visited by Europeans. The very instant I leaped on shore the collected body of natives all fell flat upon their faces, and remained in that very humble posture till, by expressive signs, I prevailed upon them to rise. They then brought a great many small pigs which they presented to me with plantain trees."

Believing Captain Cook to be the long vanished God Lono who had finally returned to Hawaii, thousands of islanders followed him about on all fours. Large quantities of pigs, potatoes, taro and coconuts were brought to the ships. In turn the Hawaiians were presented with cloth, mirrors and nails from the captain's storeroom. They were disappointed to find that when the quicksilver was scratched off the back of the glass "the picture was gone." But

[74]

nails were considered of the greatest value, since at the time of Cook's arrival the Hawaiians knew little of iron, having only a few odd bits that had been washed onto their shores in drifting wreckage. In the trading that followed, an ordinary nail bought enough fresh pork, taro and potatoes to feed the whole ship's company for a day.

Captain Cook named the group the Sandwich Islands in honor of the Earl of Sandwich, and leaving goats, sheep and vegetable seeds he sailed on to the American coast in search of the Northwest Passage. Late in November of the same year the expedition returned to the Islands and spent several weeks exploring the coasts of Maui and Hawaii. Young Kamehameha, who was already an important chief, visited both ships. At Kealakekua, on the Kona Coast, the captain was addressed by the leading priests as Lono, was honored with high temple rites, invested with the sacred red tapa cloth and allowed to kiss a sacred idol.

After the two vessels and their large crews had remained several weeks at the Island of Hawaii the drain on the island's limited resources began to tell. Chiefs were beginning to doubt the divinity of people who consumed such great quantities of pork, fruit and vegetables. The provisioning of the vessels with hundreds of pigs and tons of foodstuffs left the countryside so bare that it was finally suggested that perhaps it was time for them to leave.

"It was ridiculous," reported Lieutenant King of the *Resolution*, "to see them stroking the sides and patting the bellies of the sailors —and telling them, partly by signs and partly by words, that it was time for them to go but if they would come again the next breadfruit season they should be better able to supply our wants."

Several days after they sailed from Kealakekua they encountered a severe storm and the foremast of the *Resolution* was sprung, making it necessary to return to the bay from which they had recently departed heavily laden with gifts.

During their absence a taboo had been placed on the district to allow the people to replenish their food supplies. Consequently

[75]

there was no rejoicing among the islanders when the *Resolution* and the *Discovery* entered the bay and took up their previous anchorages. A number of small altercations occurred between the natives and the sailors, with provocation about equally divided. Finally, when the *Discovery's* cutter was stolen, Captain Cook's anger knew no bounds. He was determined to get it back at all costs and decided that the best way would be to kidnap the king and hold him as a hostage until it was returned.

The king could see no good reason to become greatly disturbed over the mere theft of a small boat, especially since the British tars had stolen a number of sacred native things. However, he agreed to go on board the *Resolution*. Captain Cook, while leading the kindly and amiable King Kalamopuu down to the beach where the ships' boats were waiting, was interrupted by the shouts of a chief.

"Heavenly one!" cried the chief, "the sea is not right! The foreigners have just killed Kilimu!"

The king's wife, hearing the tragic news, ran out to plead with him to return home. In the ensuing struggle Cook seized the king

The death of Captain Cook at Kaawaloa, Hawaii, 1779.

in an attempt to force him to the beach and precipitated a general fight in which the musket fire from his Royal Marines killed thirty Hawaiians, several of whom were high chiefs.

Captain Cook managed to regain the beach, but while waving for his boats to cease firing and come in closer he was hit on the back of the head with a club and struck in the neck with one of the iron daggers he had but recently traded to the islanders. Falling face down, in the direction and within hailing distance of his ships, the "Great Navigator" died and was carried off by the islanders. According to the custom reserved for high chiefs, the captain's bones were distributed among the nobles as sacred relics. The ribs and breastbone were placed in a temple and covered with sacred red feathers.

Despite the true greatness of Captain Cook and his best efforts to respect native rights his expedition, like that of all others that were to follow, left a broad trail of disease and general disruption at Niihau, Kauai, Oahu, Maui and Hawaii. As Kamakau, an early native historian wrote, "These are the things he planted, which sprung [sic] up and spread, bringing desolation: diseases, adultery, worship as if he were a god, fleas and mosquitos [sic], death dealing plagues, weakness of the body, changing religion and the laws of government. These things were evil and the foundation of the destruction of the people."

In 1786 the French navigator La Pérouse visited the Hawaiian Islands on a voyage of exploration. He wrote, "Although the French were the first in this present period to land on the island of Maui, I did not believe it my duty to take possession in the king's name. Doubtless philosophers must groan to see men, simply because they have cannon and bayonets, count as nothing sixty thousand of their fellows."

In 1792 when Captain George Vancouver arrived at Hawaii he brought the first young orange trees and grape vines and a quantity of garden seeds, which he distributed among the island chiefs. In return Kamehameha presented Vancouver with sugar-fattened

[77]

pigs and the island's choicest fruits. An honorable, ethical man, Vancouver was one among a very small number of early ship-masters who steadfastly refused to barter in firearms with the native chiefs. When he returned again to Hawaii from California, Vancouver brought several head of cattle which he gave to Kame-hameha. At his first sight of the cows the king was considerably concerned lest the "great hogs" should bite him. Later, when the first calf was born, the native cow grooms were so elated that they carried it on their backs for three days over the rough mountain trails to the king's residence so that Kamehameha might see the strange new creature.

Chapter four

THE FIRST AMERICANS AND KAMEHAMEHA

*T*HE FIRST AMERICAN VESSELS TO CALL AT HAWAII ARRIVED IN 1789. A group of New England merchants, inspired by the tales of John Ledyard, a Connecticut Yankee who had accompanied Captain Cook around the world, sent the *Columbia* and the *Lady Washington* around the Horn to explore the vacant lands south of the Straits of Juan de Fuca and to endeavor to establish a new field of commerce between the Northwest Pacific coast and Canton, China.

The American captains, finding that the great Hong merchants would accept only silver, opium, sharks' fins and a few other choice items, came to the Northwest Pacific for fur cargoes as a new trade medium.

After the long voyage around Cape Horn, the Boston Nor'west-men usually stopped at Hawaii where nails, chisels, red and blue cloth, molasses and ships' biscuits were traded for pigs, yams and other fresh supplies.

Most of the vessels, manned by men from Cape Cod and "down East," were small, well-built brigs, sloops and ships of sixty to two hundred tons. Averaging sixty to ninety feet in length, a size best suited for quick maneuvering in the difficult waters of the Northwest coast, all were well armed with cutlasses, muskets, swivel guns mounted on the bulwarks, and a number of cannons kept well

[79]

shotted with grape and canister. Generally they remained from one to two years along the Pacific Coast and in the Hawaiian Islands before squaring away toward Luzon and Formosa.

Prime sea-otter skins that were bought from the Indians at Nootka Sound for a six-inch-square piece of copper, or goods valued at less than a dollar in silver, were sold in China for fifty dollars each. For a return cargo, crepes, silks, nankeens, and the famed souchong, young hyson and bohea teas were carried home to Boston at a fabulous profit. Net profits of a hundred thousand dollars a voyage were not unusual. The tiny ship *Pearl* netted her owners over $206,000 in one cruise. If the skipper was a sharp trader and a two-fisted driver, as well as an able navigator and a prudent business man, in the course of a few voyages he could become a shoreside merchant prince—and many did.

American traders and super-cargoes arriving at Hawaii found that King Kamehameha I quickly learned the new ways and soon was as clever as the sharpest New Englanders. When certain traders diluted their rum with plain water and thinned the gunpowder they sold him with coal dust and ground charcoal the king promptly found it out and refused to have anything further to do with them. He proved repeatedly that he could do business according to the white man's rules and win every time.

Kamehameha, though shrewd, was honorable in dealing with white traders and captains. He extended equal trade rights to all nations without favor. He encouraged white men of skill to settle in Hawaii, and through them a large number of his people became expert carpenters, coopers, blacksmiths and tailors. White men were not allowed to own land, although they frequently received grants on condition that after death it reverted back to the king. In 1789 when the tender *Fair American* was captured by a chief's party in retaliation for the wanton slaughter of a large group of Hawaiians by Captain Metcalf of the fur ship *Eleanor,* Isaac Davis, sole survivor of the *Fair American's* crew of five, and John Young, bos'n of the *Eleanor,* were taken under the protection of Kamehameha. They were given lands with the rank of chiefs, and soon became the king's trusted advisors and generals. To "tie them to Hawaii" the king presented them with wives of high noble standing, to whom they were duly married by a visiting clergyman. Both men were intensely loyal to the king and the kingdom which

Young Hawaiians re-enact a scene from early Hawaii using priceless feather garments from Bishop Museum. The feather standards were carried before chiefs of highest rank.

they served. Later, Young became a ranking high chief of the realm and ruled over the big island of Hawaii for a decade.

Just as otter skins and sealskins brought the first white traders into the Northwest Pacific, the profits to be made in sandalwood logs attracted them regularly to Hawaii and established a thriving commerce between Honolulu and Canton. During one of Captain Kendrick's many voyages between Canton and the Pacific Coast in the ninety-ton sloop *Lady Washington* he had discovered these exotic trees growing on the island of Kauai. Impressed by its fragrance, he took a cargo of sandalwood to Canton. At first the merchants led by the great Houqua—chief of the merchants and famous throughout the trading world for his great wealth, integrity and honor—showed little interest in the new trade medium. Later, when they found that the new wood gave a fragrant scent when burned, there was a great demand for it and the Boston traders were paid one hundred and twenty-five dollars a ton for the Hawaiian logs.

Sandalwood became a three-way monopoly between the king of Hawaii, Boston's merchant adventurers and the twelve Co-hong merchants of Canton who controled all of China's import and export trade with "foreign devils." In one year alone American vessels sold nearly half a million dollars worth of sandalwood at Canton.

In 1817 Kamehameha purchased a brig named the *Kaahumanu.* He placed the vessel in charge of a white captain and sent it to China with a full cargo of sandalwood timber. More than a year later the brig returned to Hawaii loaded with bales of silk and cases of East Indian rum, and the king was greatly elated over the success of his first venture as a merchant shipowner. On going over the accounts with the captain and noticing an entry of one dollar a foot for pilotage in and out of Chinese harbors, the astute monarch promptly instructed his own pilots to charge the same price for all ships entering Hawaiian waters. In a short while the king acquired a merchant fleet of more than forty sailing vessels.

[82]

All of the prominent visitors to Hawaii were greatly impressed by their first sight of the great Kamehameha, standing nearly seven feet tall and magnificent in his classic feather helmet and flaming golden cape of mamo feathers. (It took one hundred years to collect the eighty thousand rare feathers for the king's cloak and nine generations of craftsmen to complete the six-foot-long garment.) Those who were capable of weighing natural primitive shortcomings against truly outstanding abilities were strongly impressed by his force of character, vigorous intellect, keen judgement and qualities of leadership.

Kamehameha was the equal of any of the European rulers of his day. His delightful sense of ego never allowed him to forget his own greatness. Once, in welcoming Kotzebue, he told the young Russian navigator, "I have heard that your Emperor is a great hero, and I love him for it, for I am one myself! And I send him this lei as a testimony of my regard."

It was death to stand in a position higher than the king. On one occasion when Kamehameha was on the deck of a ship and decided to go below to the captain's cabin every other Hawaiian aboard leaped instantly overboard to avoid standing at a higher elevation than the king.

When Kotzebue first arrived at Honolulu Kamehameha welcomed him in the true Hawaii manner and graciously supplied his every want, as a royal courtesy to a friendly nation.

"I learn that you are the commander of a ship of war and engaged in a voyage similar to those of Cook and Vancouver," the king told the Russian commander. "It is therefore my intention not to carry on trade with you but to provide you without obligation with everything my islands produce. This affair is now settled and no further mention may be made of it."

In showing Kotzebue the images of the sacred Hawaiian gods, Kamehameha informed him, "These are our Gods whom I worship. Whether I do right or wrong I do not know, but I follow my faith, which cannot be wicked, as it commands me never to

[83]

Heiau (ancient temple) at Kailua, Hawaii, where Kamehameha I worshipped. Queen Kaahumanu, who became regent, is shown in foreground with attendants.

do ill." Of Kamehameha Kotzebue wrote, "he only wishes to increase the happiness and not the wants of his subjects."

A shipwrecked sailor who was impressed with the king's democratic way of going about and encouraging his subjects in their work took the opportunity to tell him so.

"What? Does your king not do the same?" asked Kamehameha.

"Our king seldom goes among the people." replied the sailor, "I have never seen him."

"How then," demanded Kamehameha, "does your king know what the people want?"

Kamehameha enacted many laws to conserve the natural resources of the kingdom. The killing of cattle was forbidden for a ten-year period. Feather collectors were ordered to release all birds after plucking a few of their best feathers for cloak-making. The cutting of young sandalwood trees was forbidden and other conservation methods were taken by the foresighted monarch "so that our children may live."

[84]

Nine of the king's twenty-one wives bore him fourteen children. The highest in rank, and mother of his heirs, was the buxom Keopulani in whose august presence the great Kamehameha was accustomed to kneel. His favorite wife, the spirited and wayward Kaahumanu, was known throughout the kingdom for her radiant beauty. Daughter of a ruler of Maui, she was keenly intelligent, proud and strong, an outstanding leader in battle. At one time she was admiral of a fleet of canoes that put down a rebel uprising.

When King Kamehameha lay dying at Kailua on the Kona Coast, attended by John Young and a few others who were his closest friends, he admonished his son and successor Liholiho, "Never be hasty in punishing a fault committed by foreigners. Put up even with a second offense; only on the third should you endeavor to repel them."

Shortly after breathing his last, Kamehameha was carried to the Temple of Black Lava and laid before the altar of his gods. At sunset on May 9, 1819, while the men who had devoted their entire lives to his service were seated in a grief-stricken circle, the chanters of the mele struck the long final note to the "greatest Hawaiian."

When the time came for his son to step forth in his scarlet feather mantle and be pronounced king, Kaahumanu stood forward and said, "I make known to your highness Liholiho the will of your father. There are the guns and this is your land, but you and I will share the realm together!"

As regent she had veto powers even over the king's pronouncements. She so distinguished herself as Hawaii's first kuhina nui (regent) that the post was made permanent and written into the constitution.

In 1960, nearly a century and a half after the death of Kamehameha the First, his memory still warms the heart and stirs the national feelings of every Hawaiian. His yellow feather cape, now valued at one million dollars, is kept in a locked vault. On rare

occasions it may be seen on display at Bishop Museum in Honolulu.

Whalers and Missionaries

By the first quarter of the nineteenth century Hawaii had become a center for Pacific trade. It was not unusual to see as many
as forty vessels anchored off Honolulu on the same day. President
Monroe, recognizing the growing American interests, sent an
American "Agent for Commerce and Seamen" to the port in
1820.

While Kamehameha I had wisely conserved Hawaii's sandalwood resources, Liholiho, his son, was soon maneuvered by American merchants into such great debt that he was forced to strip the
Islands of nearly every log. His natural extravagance was encouraged and baited to such a point that he bought a whole fleet
of vessels for which he had no use, including a fifty-thousand-dol-
lar yacht.

The *Maro* of Nantucket, the first whaler to arrive at the port of
Honolulu, was soon followed by many others. With the decline
of the sandalwood and fur trades the whalers began to outnumber
the nor'westmen and the "seal skinners" at Hawaii. Lahaina, Hilo,
and Honolulu became semiannual refitting and provisioning bases for whalers operating in northern waters and as far
west as Japan. In addition, Honolulu was made a depot and
trans-shipping port for large quantities of whalebone and whale
oil.

In fitting out for a voyage to the South Pacific, whaling skippers
never shipped seamen aboard their vessels because it was impossible to obtain American sailors willing to work for the poor wages,
bad food and intolerable conditions that existed. At the beginning
of each voyage, agents in New York, Buffalo, Philadelphia and
other cities distributed romantic handbills depicting the lure of

BOKI.
GOVERNOR OF WAHU, OF THE SANDWICH ISLANDS,
AND HIS WIFE
LILIHA.

*High Chief Boki and his wife Liliha. Boki accompanied King Liholiho Kame-
hameha II to London in 1824.*

Hawaii and the South Seas, the large profits, and the thrill of chasing whales that invariably attracted young city and farm boys. They were told by the agents that their slightest wish would be respected, that they would have "yer choice of a whole pumpkin or mince pie twice per day." Before signing they were assured that the captain would treat them as though they were his own sons and give them all the shore liberty they wished when they reached the tropics.

The young boys who shipped soon found they were roundly flogged for the slightest infractions of shipboard routine. After long months of living on "hogwash and hardtack," of curses from the mates and bruises from the rope's-end, of seeing their few dollars in wages absorbed by the captain in return for the advance of a jacket and a few pounds of raw tobacco from the slop chest, most were only too glad to see the last of the vessel immediately upon arrival at Honolulu.

In 1826 when Captain Thomas Catesby Jones arrived in Hawaii to protect commerce and induce American sailors to join ships in need of their services, he found thousands of seamen "on the beach" at Honolulu. Four years later the crew problem had become so bad that Consul Jones recommended semiannual visits of American warships "to reduce desertions and mutinies, and to punish the guilty."

Several of the most infamous whaling masters—men known from coast to coast as cold-blooded fiends on the quarter-deck—posed as pious churchmen while at Hawaii, and even made sizeable donations to the missions to gain the aid of the missionaries in securing natives to replace the many white men who deserted their ships.

The first Hawaiians to ship as sailors aboard homeward-bound whalers caused a considerable stir upon their arrival at New Haven. They were taken in hand by a group of Yale theological students and later held up as inspiring examples of the great need for a mission school. When the American Board of Commissioners for Foreign Missions established a special school for native converts at Cornwall, Connecticut, the young Hawaiians were among the first nine pupils. Their tales of paganism and of the worship of idols aroused the devout puritans of Connecticut and Massachusetts to thinking about the sad plight of native sinners. When a fund was proposed to save the Hawaiian race from "the dangerous shoals of damnation" contributions literally poured in. Prominent New England families who had accumulated large fortunes in the rum and slave trade were among the first and the largest contributors.

Shortly after the death of Kamehameha I the brig *Thaddeus* sailed from Boston with a group of fourteen young newlyweds, fresh out of college and eager to tame the savage heathen. On their arrival at Kailua Bay the evangelists found much to complain about. Even before they landed, Reverend Bingham reports, "The appearance of almost naked savages, whose heads and feet, and much of their sunburned, swarthy skins, were bare, was appalling. Some of our number, with gushing tears, turned away from the spectacle."

Surrounded by scores of handsome, joyous natives, many of whom stood six feet tall in their healthy, naked state, others of the missionary party questioned, "Can these be human beings? Can such beings be civilized?" The missionary wives had special complaints, for after the long salt water voyage there were months of accumulated washing to do "in a heathen brook." And to clothe the buxom Hawaiian females against the "lustful gaze of males" required long gowns and a tremendous amount of needlework. The average weight of a female chief was recorded at three hundred pounds and Bingham's strict orders were to "have it come down to their toes."

The dissolute King Liholiho, fearing that the men with the black box (Bible) might attempt to deprive him of four of his

[89]

five wives, was reluctant to give permission for them to remain long in the Islands. It took twelve days of Brother Bingham's most ardent rhetoric and the aid of Kamehameha's old friend John Young before the missionaries were granted permission to stay for one year. They were then presented with houses, gardens, furniture and servants.

When the first school was set up, the king and all of the members of the royal family became the most ardent pupils. They felt that "if the palapala (the written word) is a good thing, we must have it first, for it is not right that a people know more than their rulers." To provide a sounding board for his Christianity and to let others know that he had become a highly educated ruler, Kuakini, the governor of Kona, built the first Christian church in the Islands and, as deacon, saw to it that any woman who entered without a bonnet had her hair shaved off in punishment. The attention of the congregation was assured by several policemen on the lookout throughout the services to rap sleepers on the head with a long cane.

During their first year in the group the missionaries devoted themselves wholeheartedly to the uprooting of sin and, according to their own records, were highly successful. Most of the old taboos and religious beliefs were abolished. Great, beautiful idols that would be the pride of any museum today were smashed to bits, burned, or tossed off of high windward cliffs.

Through the good offices of John Young and others Liholiho came to regard the missionaries as a necessary part of his realm, so far as his subjects were concerned. In putting off his own conversion to the church the king explained to the Reverend Bingham, "My sins are as thick as ohelo berries. How can you expect me to drop them all at once? Why don't you go after some of my chiefs who are already fairly good men? They haven't much to give up. My own wickedness is too great. In five years I will forsake sin."

"You must do it now," Reverend Bingham warned the king.

"Even five months or five days may be too late. Repent now, this very hour, if you want to save your soul."

"Brother Bingham," replied his majesty politely but firmly, "I've heard you missionaries say 'one thing at a time.' That is how I have decided to drop my sins—one at a time. In five years I shall be a good man."

Queen Kaahumanu, the real power behind the throne, regarded the puritans with a wary eye. Not taken in by glowing sermons and rosy promises, she decided to wait a few years and judge by the results that were accomplished. In the meantime, while outwardly civil, she demanded full respect for her royal position and usually in shaking hands with missionaries or their wives extended only her little finger. A number of years later, when the queen decided to "accept religion," she became outstanding in church work and admonished her subjects to obey the edicts of the Boston puritans.

Dancing came to be strictly forbidden. The true Hawaiian hula was a sacred dance that combined history, religion and poetry. Islanders danced the story of the coconut tree and the breadfruit tree. They danced the natural history of the land and sea. Dancers also told the stories of their people. Now the Boston puritans told them this was sinful and must be stopped.

Missionary efforts among the common people were successful and in ten years' time more than forty thousand natives were receiving religious instruction. When the missionary-historian Ellis visited the group he was able to report that the Sabbath was observed with the greatest decorum. "No athletic sports were seen on the beach, nor any canoes passing across the calm surface of the bay; no noise of playful children shouting as they gamboled in the surf, nor distant sound of the cloth-beating mallet was heard throughout the day; it could be viewed as the dawn of a bright sabbatic day for the dark shores of Hawaii."

Years later when Mark Twain visited Hawaii he was so struck by the hold religion had gained and still held over the natives as to write, "They all belong to the church and are fonder of theology than they are of pie; they will sweat out a sermon as long as the Declaration of Independence; the duller it is the more it infatuates them."

The natural enmity among the American merchants, sailors and missionaries eventually involved all the white population in the bitterest kind of rivalry. The white residents were the first to complain that the missionaries were depriving the people of their harmless amusements and making them into "hypocritical, Bible-quoting fops." An early American consular agent wrote that the missionaries were not only "living like lords in this luxurious land" but were disturbing the minds of these children of nature with the idea that they are to be eternally damned unless they think and act as they do." The British consular agent added that he could see no hope for the Hawaiians under a regime which combined "the blue laws of Connecticut with the tyranny of a Turkish Pasha."

In 1839 the French frigate *L'Artémise* blockaded Honolulu harbor and threatened an immediate bombardment unless all restrictions against Catholicism and against French wines and brandies were removed. The Hawaiians and their missionary advisors had no choice but to accept the ultimatum. They were required to post a bond of twenty thousand piasters against future intolerance or discrimination.

By 1839 American missionaries were taking an increasing interest in Hawaii's temporal as well as spiritual affairs. In that year they persuaded mild and impressionable King Kamehameha III to relinguish much of his power, to grant a Bill of Rights and to create a legislative body. Ten years later the best official positions and judgeships were held by Americans—several of whom were ex-missionaries who had forsaken the cloth for political careers.

In Boston, the Mission Board maintained a vigilant watch and exerted its full influence at Washington to see that the right diplomats were sent out to Hawaii. The Reverend Armstrong once wrote from Honolulu, "When a new President comes in, can you not stir yourselves and send us either a good consul general or a good commissioner?" Commodore Downes of the United States frigate *Potomac* felt it necessary to advise the missionaries bluntly that they should concentrate on helping the natives and leave trade and government affairs to others.

King Kamehameha III, acting on the advice of Dr. Judd, a former missionary, repealed the law against permitting foreigners to own land. At the same time about a third of the royal holdings were handed over to the commoners to do with as they saw fit. White residents had long been urging such a law. They extended credit immediately to all native landholders who desired it and urged it on those who did not. In a relatively short time a number of choice native holdings were obtained by local white merchants, missionaries and others by foreclosure on land mortgages. Many Hawaiians forfeited their land on a game of chance; others exchanged it for a few yards of colored cloth. One way or another, while the Islanders were concentrating on learning the three R's, reading Bunyan's *Pilgrims Progress* and memorizing long passages from the *Bible,* much of their best seashore and valley land was coming under white ownership.

As early as 1852 evangelists were purchasing thousands of acres of the best lands in Hawaii for fifty-six cents an acre. A number of these large tracts became the cornerstones by which their descendants rose to be the first families of Hawaii. Although the first missionaries had, besides piety, a highly developed property sense, it remained for their sons to see the real money-making possibilities. The sons took over their fathers' lands and eventually went into factoring, shipping and banking, occupations at which they were as ingenious and successful as their Yankee fathers had been at proselytizing. In a surprisingly short time they controlled far more of Hawaii than the native Hawaiians. As the young Hawaiians tell it, "the sons of missionaries acquired the land and left the natives holding the Bible."

By 1840 the prosperous American colony at Honolulu had become the most important American outpost in the Pacific. Its merchants controlled much of the mercantile business in California and Oregon coastal ports. Its newspapers were widely read along the Pacific west coast and a large number of coastal residents sent their children to be educated in Honolulu schools. Although San Francisco succeeded Honolulu as the commercial center of the northeastern Pacific, the Hawaiian crossroads maintained its importance as a port of call and trading center for the eastern Pacific. It was frequently said of Yankee skippers in the Pacific that they could sell coconuts to the natives, and one or two actually did. In the forties Captain Samuel Kennedy of the merchant ship *Izar* of Boston sold a varied cargo at Honolulu that included tombstones, codfish, umbrellas and palm-leaf hats!

King Kamehameha III, noting with alarm the growth of American commercial and political influence in his domain, sent a Hawaiian delegation to Washington in 1842 to request a formal recognition of Hawaiian independence—a recognition which President Tyler and Secretary of State Daniel Webster endeavored to evade. After waiting eight days for an answer the Hawaiian representatives threatened that, in the event the United States persisted in refusing their request, they would proceed to London without further delay and request a British protectorate. This goaded the President to immediate action and on December 30 he informed Congress that the United States would view with dissatisfaction any action by another power which violated the independence of the Hawaiian kingdom.

Dudoit, the French Consul, lamenting the tendency of the American missionaries to amass commercial and political power, forewarned his government that unless the commanders of French warships took a stronger attitude Hawaii would soon be taboo for all foreigners who did not agree with the missionaries' religious beliefs.

[94]

By 1850 the activities of the French and the ever-increasing trade between Honolulu and the Pacific Coast ports prompted repeated appeals from local missionaries, merchants and others for more attention from the State Department. California's fast-expanding population and the booming Gold Rush days created a large demand for Hawaiian foodstuffs. The forty-niners bought all the potatoes, sugar, beans, squash and fruit that the Islands could send them. Scores of vessels arrived at San Francisco with cargoes of potatoes that sold for eight dollars a bushel and sugar at ten cents a pound wholesale.

Traders and merchants proudly claimed that under the stimulating effects of commerce and trade native Hawaiians had made "an absolute leap toward civilization." Nevertheless they were determined not to allow any "prattle about native rights" to stand in the way of business expansion. Acting to increase their personal interests, as early as 1853 a militant-minded group of Americans calling themselves the Committee of Thirteen were threatening "revolution and a republic." In the same year the Reverend William Alexander wrote "Perhaps Hawaii may be . . . the 32nd star in our national ensign. We would then be out of the reach of insults from the French. On the other hand, however, the native Hawaiian race would be trampled in the dust . . . therefore I wish not to be annexed and pray it may never be consummated."

Despite their narrowness, intolerance and—in many cases—severe and oppressive attitudes, the missionaries, together with a few political-adventurers, were almost the only Americans in Hawaii who sincerely devoted themselves over a long period of time to doing what they thought to be in the best interests of the native people. The merchants and traders were most concerned with their own balance sheets, consular agents with their personal ambitions and seamen with their pleasures. In a surprisingly short time the missionaries reduced the native language to writing, translated and printed the Bible in Hawaiian and estab-

[95]

lished the first school system. They introduced various health and sanitation measures, taught vocational crafts and earnestly sought to raise the living standards of the common people. Whatever might be said of their intolerance—and much can—their courage, devotion and sincerity must remain unquestioned.

Chapter five

LAST OF THE HAWAIIAN KINGDOM

*A*T A TIME WHEN WHALING WAS BEGINNING TO DECLINE, LARGELY because of the discovery of petroleum, the fast-growing populations of California and Oregon were demanding more sugar than Hawaii could produce. With the outbreak of the Civil War and the disruption of the sugar industry in the southern states the demand became so great that the price of Hawaiian cane sugar leaped from four cents to as high as twenty-five cents per pound. In 1867 the establishment of steamship service between San Francisco and China greatly increased transportation facilities between Hawaii and the United States. Despite competition from the Philippines, the production of sugar soon took the place of whaling as the territory's principal industry. Hawaiian sugar, because of its fine quality, continued to be on demand in the American market and generally brought a cent a pound more than all other imported types.

As early as 1802 a Chinese farmer on the island of Lanai had been growing "the honey-bearing grass" and processing it in a crude stone mill operated by hand. There had been a number of others in the early nineteenth century, but it remained for Ladd and Company, an American firm with a small plantation on the island of Kauai, to make the first important effort to manufacture sugar on a commercial scale.

By 1853 Americans were cultivating several thousand acres of cane. There were many problems to be solved. Most important were labor, water, and the elimination of insect pests.

An average cane stalk is composed of seventy-two percent water, eighteen percent sugar, and about ten percent fibre. Therefore a vast amount of water is required—two thousand pounds of it for every pound of sugar. Green sugar cane leaves combine carbon dioxide from the air with elements of water drawn up by the plant's roots and convert them into sugar. (Chlorophyl, the substance that makes the leaves of all plants green, is what puts the sugar into the sap of sugar plants. To do its job well chlorophyl requires lots of strong sunshine.)

Many "hapai ko" (carry-cane) laborers were required to till the ground, cut the cane and transport it to the mill. Much of the pioneering work was done by native Hawaiians. They cleared the land, built ditches, planted, cultivated, harvested the cane and did the heavy work in the mills. As it was the most arduous kind of labor, the Hawaiians refused to work for less than twenty-five cents per day.

When it began to look as though large profits were assured the planters decided to expand, and decided too that an assured supply of cheap, docile coolies was necessary and much to be preferred to the fast-dwindling, still slightly independent remnants of the Hawaiian race. In 1852 a group of Chinese coolies from Canton were the first of several hundred thousand laborers to be brought in from the Far East during the first century of organized sugar production. In addition to their daily rice and a barn to sleep in, the Chinese were paid two cents an hour for a ten to twelve hour day. Many committed suicide. Others, as soon as their indentures expired (usually in five years), became small shopkeepers, artisans and truck gardeners. Some married natives and acquired small property holdings.

In the early eighties when the great influx of Orientals threatened to absorb the Hawaiians and create a Hawaii controlled by Asiatics, American Secretary of State Blaine declared that the

Hawaiian Archipelago "cannot be joined to the Asiatic system. If they drift from their independent state it must be toward assimilation and identification with the American system to which they belong by the operation of natural laws and must belong by the operation of political necessity." Strongly in favor of a policy of colonization and material exploitation, Secretary Blaine instructed the United States Minister at Hawaii to endeavor to obtain the passage of homestead laws that would favor emigrants and encourage American colonists to settle in the Islands.

During the reign of King Kalakaua an increasingly large number of foreigners, mostly Americans, actively interfered in the affairs of the Hawaiian government. The jolly king was entertained nightly and encouraged in his gambling by American business men, political adventurers and land speculators who were always ready to oblige with large loans in exchange for rich sugar lands or other lucrative concessions.

The young, lusty sugar industry, seeking special privileges calculated to attract sugar capital, demanded and received government support for a proposed reciprocity treaty between Hawaii and the United States. King Kalakaua was sent to Washington flanked by a host of American "advisors" to plead the case for the sugar interests. There was strong opposition in the United States Senate to such a treaty. It was pointed out that such a bill would benefit a small handful of Americans and the Hawaiian royal family to the disadvantage of the majority of the native people, who would be still further relegated to the odd, rocky corners·of their islands to make room for the great cane fields and the Oriental masses—who would in turn create a peonage system.

The sugar "advisors" let it be known in Washington that unless they were granted full economic preference, they would ship their entire crop to Australia, New Zealand and British Columbia in the future years. The implication was obvious. In such an event, the United States would lose the Hawaiian trade and the

[99]

These tassels at the tops of sugar cane reach a height of twenty feet or more in less than two years.

Islands would be certain to drift toward Great Britain politically. The veiled threat was effective, and a Reciprocity Treaty was signed in 1876 granting the Hawaiian sugar planters the privilege of exporting their sugar to the United States duty free.

The real rise of Hawaii's missionary-merchant-planter aristocracy might be said to date from this Reciprocity Treaty which opened the boom era in sugar. It was in that same year that Alexander and Baldwin, the sons of missionaries, completed the

[100]

famous Hamakua Ditch on Maui, which poured forty million gallons of water daily into the vast lowland plains, turning them from a hot, dry area into fertile sugar lands.

The factors, or middlemen, many of whom began their careers as merchants providing supplies to the whalers and mercantile products to the people of Hawaii, turned to acting as agents for the ninety sugar plantations. Gradually they assumed control—first, of finance, then of the importation of labor, and the purchase of equipment, and finally of the sales and distribution. For two and one-half percent of a planter's gross income, the factoring company took over the administration of purchasing, marketing, shipping and labor supply problems.

By astute management the factors put system and stability into the industry. Scouts were sent to scour the labor marts of Asia and within a six-year period beginning in 1880 nearly fifty thousand Chinese and Japanese coolie laborers were imported. Since the planters were guaranteed a duty-free market for all the sugar they could produce, in the first ten years following the Reciprocity Treaty production increased fivefold and sugar stocks soared sky high. However, in 1890 when the McKinley Tariff Bill was put into effect, placing raw sugar on the free list and granting a two cent per pound bounty to domestic producers, a severe depression resulted in Hawaii. The factors, ready and financially able to seize upon this sudden development to institute their own field management, took over at small cost the many privately owned plantations that were forced to the wall.

King Kalakaua, who ruled Hawaii from 1874 to 1891, was a strong believer in a Hawaii ruled by and for the Hawaiians. The big planters, factoring companies, and other American business interests were, naturally, decidedly opposed to this point of view and would have much preferred a constitutional monarchy with the king relegated to the handling of social events while their own appointees made and controlled the laws of the land. By 1887 the foreign white residents were already in control of the legislature and in one way or another were always able to bring strong pressure to bear upon the cabinet ministers.

On a number of occasions when the cabinet ministers became too obviously pro-American the king promptly dismissed them, as was his right under the constitution of 1864. This, of course, was strongly resented by the New Englanders who were already in control of most of the land and all of the business. In June, 1887, they forced King Kalakaua to agree to a revised constitution. Under the guise of creating a democratic, parliamentary form of government, the new constitution provided that the legislators should henceforth be elected. It also provided that only those who had property could vote. Since four-fifths of all the property in the Islands was, at that time, already owned by whites of foreign birth or ancestry, foreign property owners came into immediate control of the newly "elected" parliament.

In 1891 King Kalakaua suddenly died while on a visit to the Pacific Coast and Princess Liliuokalani ascended the throne. The new ruler was a widely-traveled woman of high culture and talents. During her lifetime she composed over a hundred songs, including "Aloha Oe," known around the world as the symbol of Hawaii. She was fair-minded, capable and decidedly nationalistic. The pathetic story of the cultured queen, nobly striving to retain the dignity and sovereignty of her island government against a small but bitterly determined band of American opportunists, is the final chapter in the drama of two nationalities—Hawaiian and American—struggling for the control of Hawaii.

Queen Liliuokalani, in a vain attempt to curb the foreign domination that had spread like a thundercloud, proposed several constitutional amendments incorporating the principle of "Hawaii for the Hawaiians." Most important was the proposal to limit voting to the citizens of the kingdom so that foreign property owners could no longer dominate the government.

An underground organization including many well-known

Hulihee Palace, on the Kona Coast of the Island of Hawaii, was the summer residence of King Kalakaua.

business men had been waiting for just such an event. In the words of one of the members, the queen's proposals offered them "a splendid opportunity to get rid of the old regime." Under the disarming title of a "Committee for Safety" they acquired ammunition, rifles and other small arms. The American Minister, John L. Stevens, met privately with the revolutionists and agreed to send marines from the *U.S.S. Boston* under the guise of protecting American property. The evening of January 16, 1893 became a night of terror in Honolulu. Fires of unexplained origin broke out and many Islanders fled to the safety of the mountains. The following afternoon the Americans, backed by well-placed riflemen, seized the treasury and proclaimed the overthrow of the Hawaiian queen.

Liliuokalani had long been helpless, since her cabinet, composed mainly of Americans, had openly defied her will and refused to carry out her requests. Her Minister of the Interior had received orders from the revolutionary committee to defy the queen. With United States Marines parading through the town, the queen had no choice but to surrender. Liliuokalani made it quite plain that she "surrendered to the superior forces of the United States of America, whose minister has caused United States troops to be landed at Honolulu." Although backed wholeheartedly by her people, who naturally resented seeing a group of whites overthrow their monarch, the queen issued a signed statement agreeing "to yield my authority until such time as the Government of the United States shall, upon the facts presented to it, undo the action of its representative and reinstate me in the authority which I claim as the constitutional sovereign of the Hawaiian Islands."

The revolutionists, calling themselves the Provisional Government, shrewdly prevailed upon the conservative and somewhat reluctant Judge Sanford Dole to remain as their head and sent a delegation to Washington to demand annexation. The delegates felt that they could rely on the Southern Democrats with their racial attitudes to understand and rally to the support of Hawaii's small but dominant white ruling caste. In the meantime, Minister Stevens, acting without authorization from his superiors, declared an American protectorate over Hawaii.

President Grover Cleveland, alarmed by the international storm that was brewing over the highhanded events at Honolulu, withdrew the annexation treaty from the Senate.

"It would lower our national standards to endorse a selfish and dishonorable scheme of a lot of adventurers," declared Secretary of State John Gresham. Later the Secretary wrote, "I am opposed to annexation, especially of territory not a part of our continent. If I were in favor of annexation, however, I should oppose taking the islands by force and fraud . . . I think there is such a thing as international morality." Thomas F. Bayard, American Ambassador to London, was moved to write, "Our country is too great and aspires to too high a place in civilization to stoop to the small arts of tricking and bullying a scanty and feeble set of islanders out of their rights." In Congress, Senator Mills of Texas asked, "Is that day coming when along Pennsylvania Avenue we shall see a Hawaiian Queen, weighted down with sugar sacks on her back, pleading in behalf of her people for the right to institute a government for themselves?"

James H. Blount, former Chairman of the House Foreign Affairs Committee, was sent to Hawaii as special commissioner to ascertain the true facts about the revolution. After a long and impartial investigation Blount reported back to President Cleveland that the popular queen had been overthrown by a well-planned conspiracy between the disgruntled opportunists and Minister Stevens with the free use of United States troops. The Commissioner also informed the President that the revolution could not have succeeded without the collusion and aid of Minister Stevens, as "the undoubted sentiment of the people is for the queen, against the Provisional Government and against annexation."

[105]

Queen Liliuokalani, the last monarch of Hawaii, wrote the poignant, most be-loved of Hawaiian songs, **Aloha Oe,** *while under arrest at Iolani Palace.*

Amazed to hear that the American minister had taken part in destroying the native dynasty, President Cleveland discarded the treaty of annexation, stating, "I mistake the American people if they favor the odious doctrine that there is no such thing as international morality; that there is one law for the strong and one for the weak."

Albert S. Willis was appointed United States Minister and sent to inform Queen Liliuokalani that President Cleveland would restore her to the throne providing she would grant full pardon to the revolutionists. The proud queen pointed out that according to Hawaiian law Thurston, the ringleader, should be beheaded; but she was willing to forgive and forget, and gave the American minister an official pledge of amnesty for all.

When Minister Willis called upon the leaders of the so-called Provisional Government to disband and return to their former occupations, they refused point blank and chose, instead, to defy the President of the United States in the same manner that they had previously defied the will of the Queen of Hawaii. When the Americans persisted in ignoring President Cleveland's wishes there was little that could be done short of ordering a warship to enforce his instructions, a procedure which would have caused strong feelings at home, especially among the Southern Democrats. The revolutionists were well aware that their defiance had placed the President in a decidedly embarrassing position and that, on that account alone, there was little chance of annexation in the immediate future. Not daring to submit their administration to a plebiscite of the Hawaiian people, the militant group established a minority government on July 4, 1894, termed the Republic of Hawaii.

With the establishment of the Republic the foreign element came into complete political and economic control of the Islands. The sugar interests, although fearing congressional reaction to their importation of indentured labor, were anxious to bring their sugar lands within American jurisdiction where they would enjoy sugar bounties. In this, they continued to encounter strong opposition within the United States.

The outbreak of the Spanish-American War immediately cast the Hawaiian situation in a new light. The strategic value of the Islands for military and naval purposes was recognized and admitted by all factions. An annexation bill was hurried through the Senate and the House of Representatives and Hawaii officially became a part of the United States on August 12, 1898.

Rise of Sugar and Pineapples

By the turn of the century the Hawaiian sugar industry had entered a new era. Ninety plantations had joined together to form the Hawaiian Sugar Planters' Association. Scientists were hired and sent around the world to gather specimens and the latest sugar cane data. An experimental laboratory was set up and thousands of seedlings were imported from foreign countries. Plant diseases and pest threats were eradicated.

Once, when a scourge of cane borers threatened to wipe out the industry, years of research were undertaken in the jungles of South America, in the Indies and Australia until an insect was found that would destroy the borer without harming the sugar cane. When leaf hoppers became a menace a tiny insect was brought up from Australia to destroy the leaf hoppers' eggs. A dangerous beetle was routed by a fierce little wasp brought over from the Philippines. To keep down insects, a large toad that relishes even scorpions and centipedes was brought in from Puerto Rico.

Pollen was shaken from one cane bloom into another to produce new varieties of sugar stock. From thousands of plants one occasionally stood out as does a champion among men. One vigorous strain labeled "H-109" produced enough cane per acre to make fourteen tons of sugar. Plants and field conditions were improved until single acres were made to yield as much as one hundred tons of cane.

[108]

As sugar emerged into the bracket of big business a new generation came into control. Some of the managers were sons of the pioneers, who had gone to mainland universities and then returned to the Islands to enter business. Under their direction mountain streams were diverted from their courses and taken through flumes and waterways to the lowlands. Marsh areas were drained and transformed into rich fields of sugar cane blooming ten to twenty feet high. New machinery was brought in and ingenious new devices were designed to heighten efficiency. To protect watersheds they introduced trees from all over the world, planting millions and broadcasting seeds by plane. New harbors were laid out and old ones improved, and a great transportation network was built with flumes, roads and nine hundred miles of plantation railroads.

Hawaii's annual sugar production rose to a million tons by 1932. As sugar mounted in importance other Island industries sprung up. The phenomenal growth of the pineapple industry from a few tons of half wild "pines" in 1878 to a fifty-million-dollar crop by 1930 was fully as remarkable as the development of sugar.

No one is certain just when or how the first pineapple got to Hawaii. Pineapples are believed to be native to Brazil. Some believe that they were brought by the earliest traders from America, where they were first discovered by Columbus.

Whalers and merchantmen took on an occasional cargo of a small, wild variety of pineapple that had begun to flourish along the Kona Coast as early as 1850. Whenever a fast vessel was sailing from Honolulu for the Pacific Coast in the month of June, a small shipment of "pines" was frequently sent along, consigned to San Francisco, where they had become popular during the gold rush days. Shipments increased toward the close of the century but it was found that a large percentage spoiled before reaching their destination. In 1892 Captain Kidwell, a pioneer who had started the first plantation and imported the best plants from

Jamaica, opened the first pineapple cannery. Twelve years later James Dole set up a modern cannery and organized the Hawaiian Pineapple Company, Ltd.

A pineapple plantation does not require nearly as much capital outlay as a sugar plantation. For one thing, expensive irrigation projects are not required. Pineapples need but little moisture and irrigation is unnecessary. They do well on the higher elevations unsuited to sugar raising and their labor requirements are less. Nevertheless, the early industry was beset with many problems unknown to the sugar industry. A Pineapple Producers' Cooperative Association was organized which was similar to the Hawaiian Sugar Planters' Association. Parasites were introduced to destroy domestic insects that were harmful to pineapple plants. A new spray was devised to prevent the plants from turning yellow. Plant diseases and fungi were overcome. An iron sulphate spray was developed to supply iron to plants that need it, and hormone sprays to hasten or retard ripening. Through improved field methods and experimental research a single acre of red volcanic soil could be enriched to produce as much as thirty-five tons in a single crop.

Nearly all of the complicated machinery and canning processes had to be devised and developed for the first time. An amazing machine invented by Henry Ginaca in 1913 enabled the industry to swing into mass production. The Ginaca machine, receiving pineapples as fast as one hundred and twenty a minute, peels off the outer shell, pares the fruit into a smooth cylinder, punches out the core, slices off the top and bottom, then scrapes as much fruit pulp as possible from the shell.

When the agricultural and mechanical problems were overcome there was the important problem of a market. Unlike sugar, pineapples were—and still are—considered a luxury item. A large demand had to be created. Under the aggressive leadership of James D. Dole large-scale advertising and mass distribution methods were put into effect. From twelve acres the industry expanded its area to eighty thousand acres of fragrant, gray-green pineapple

A Ginaca machine removes the shell and core and cuts off the ends of one hundred pineapples a minute.

fields, and from a hand-operated canning plant it progressed to the world's largest cannery. By 1930 Hawaii was producing four-fifths of the world's pineapples and they stood a close second to sugar for leadership in the territorial economy.

Soon after the annexation of Hawaii the United States Congress ordered Hawaii's system of indentured labor abolished, a system that Secretary of State Fish had once called "but the slave trade under another name." Thousands of sugar laborers, on learning for the first time that they were free to come and go as they wished and to work for whomever they pleased, left the plantations for jobs in Honolulu or to return to their native lands. Between 1902 and 1907 forty thousand Japanese left the Hawaiian Islands for California. A good many of those who remained on the plantations engaged in demonstrations and strikes to have their wages raised from five cents to seven cents per hour.

Although not unexpected, the sudden loss of their penal labor contracts struck the sugar planters a major blow. Claus Spreckles, California's sugar king who controlled the market and price of Hawaiian sugar, fought hard against the abolishment order and declared emphatically that "sugar production can not be carried on profitably without an abundance of cheap, humble labor." At an early sugar planters' convention it was candidly affirmed that "the experience of sugar growing the world over goes to prove that cheap labor, which means in plain words servile labor, must be employed in order to render this enterprise successful." Overnight, the problem of acquiring and holding an adequate supply of inexpensive cane choppers and mill workers became the industry's greatest concern.

During the first three decades of the new century more than three hundred thousand Japanese and Filipinos were brought across the Pacific, to outnumber the Hawaiians more than four to one. By the time of annexation there were forty-six thousand Chinese in the islands. Then, with China closed as a labor supply by the discriminatory Chinese Exclusion Act, the planters turned to Nippon and by 1907 more than one hundred and eighty thousand Japanese had been shipped in. By 1913 eighteen thousand Portuguese were recruited in Madeira and the Azores.

In its endless quest, the Hawaiian Sugar Planters' Association sent scouts to Puerto Rico, Korea, Russia, Germany, Norway and Spain. Over twenty-five thousand workers were sent back from those countries. Finally, labor rustlers were sent out to the populous Philippines and one hundred and twenty thousand Filipinos passed in through the Port of Honolulu and were sent out to work in the pineapple fields and to help harvest and crush the heavy, juice-filled cane stalks on Oahu, Maui, Hawaii and Kauai.

In 1919 the Federation of Japanese Labor in Hawaii sent a resolution to the sugar planters requesting a wage increase from seventy-seven cents to one dollar and twenty-five cents per day and a minimum of ninety-five cents a day for women laborers. In brief, their resolution stated, "We are laborers working on the sugar plantations of Hawaii. We consider it a great privilege and pride to live under the Stars and Stripes—as a factor of this great industry.

"Fifty years ago, when we first came to Hawaii, these islands were covered with ohia forests, guava fields, and areas of wild grass. Day and night did we work, cutting trees and burning grass, clearing lands and cultivating fields until we made the plantations what they are today. Of course, it is indisputable that this would have been impossible if it were not for the investments made and the untiring efforts of the administrators.

"People know Hawaii as the Paradise of the Pacific and as a sugar-producing country, but do they know that there are thousands of laborers in field and factory who are under ten hours of hard labor for seventy-seven cents a day?

"Look at the silent tombstones in every locality. Few are the people who visit these graves of our departed friends, but are they not emblems of Hawaii's pioneers in labor?"

[113]

So far as the native Hawaiian was concerned he had long been a forgotten man politically and economically. Unlike the Maoris and the Fijians who had their land rights protected for them by the British and New Zealand governments, the native Hawaiians were allowed to become economic orphans in their own abundant isles. With sugar and pineapples taking up ninety-five per cent of the available land, the Hawaiian had but one choice: he could labor as a drudge on a giant plantation or he could eke out an existence on the fringe of the coffee and pineapple lands or in the shadow of the great cane fields, as many did in Kauai and along the Kona Coast of Hawaii. The choice didn't seem to make much difference. Native culture had long since disappeared. Native arts and crafts were to be seen, if at all, in a museum. Their population had tumbled over sixty percent in less than fifty years. The Hawaiians knew the bell was tolling for their race. "Na ohipakahi ia aku nei e ka pa," their elders expressed it—"One by one they have gone into the darkness."

Chapter six

TOWARD STATEHOOD

$\mathcal{T}$HE NET RETURNS OF THE SUGAR AND PINEAPPLE PLANTATIONS continued to increase through low wages, efficient management and sound financing. At the same time they were gradually brought under central control. Ninety sugar plantations were consolidated and reduced to thirty-five companies. Thirty-four of the companies representing over ninety-six percent of the total sugar production came into the hands of five factoring agents who also acquired control over five of the eight pineapple companies.

The Big Five

The Big Five, closely bound by intermarriage, by inheritance and by an inner circle of directorates, began early to act as one in politics, labor relations and social legislation. By pyramiding their holdings, about fifteen men acquired a centralized control that extended to every important part of Island economy. Fast-mounting surplus capital from sugar and pineapple lands was used to branch out into many industries, as well as trust companies, Honolulu's two main banks, and its largest department store. Their wholesale and retail chains handled more than ninety percent of the Territory's total retail business in all lines from toothbrushes to automobiles. Their many holdings gave them the Islands' biggest insurance business.

[115]

If a citizen of Honolulu turned his radio to a local program he listened to a Big Five station. If he rode to town on a streetcar and went to a theater he patronized two more Big Five enterprises. When he took a drink of water, turned on the gas or electricity or made a telephone call he did business with three of the Big Five public utilities.

Spokesmen for the Big Five held that the Territory never could have realized its highly developed economy and great wealth without centralized control. Specifically they claimed that, because of the huge investments necessary for research and the unstable marketing conditions, the sugar and pineapple industries required their own sound financing and dominant mass production techniques. On a group of islands located two thousand miles from the nearest mainland city, they assert, it is necessary to bring forward a simultaneous development of such allied industries as transportation, purchasing, marketing, and banking. If one failed to keep pace, all would suffer. Today they point, too, to their many social services and to the Territory's achievements in education, and challenge comparison with any other semitropical agricultural area. Accustomed to being singled out as the Big Five, yet still annoyed by the phrase, the families declare that their grandfathers were hard-working sea captains, traders, missionaries, planters, bookkeepers; that their fortunes were made in the normal way, after seventy years of enterprise and vision. They feel that the development of their empire was a typically American achievement.

A strong middle class, representing a number of different nationalities, emerged during the nineteen thirties to take an active part in the financial as well as the political and social life of the Territory. Well-educated island-born children of Japanese, Chinese, Puerto Rican, Portuguese, Filipino and Hawaiian parentage graduated from Island high schools and from the University of Hawaii. A number started small businesses of their own. Others became craftsmen, accountants, doctors, teachers, mechanics, lawyers, newspaper men, or druggists. Their eyes were open. They saw things in Hawaii that were different from the democratic ideals they had read about in school. They also saw that while many of their relatives and classmates were unable to find jobs in the "land of opportunity" the sugar interests were still endeavoring to bring in thousands of additional Filipino workers.

After being educated to American standards few of the younger island-born generation cared to work in the cane fields. Those who did "lost face" among their fellows. It just didn't seem to make sense to spend eight to twelve years obtaining an American education in order to chop cane at twenty-five cents an hour. Articles appeared in a number of small independent newspapers deploring conditions in the sugar and pineapple industries and the lack of opportunity and advancement for young, Island-educated men and women. Citizens' associations began to campaign for an American standard of living for everyone. The first important labor union appeared. New organizations were formed with the avowed purpose of seeing that a few legislators not representing the Big Five were elected to office. The president of the University of Hawaii, Dr. David Crawford, warned that while "rugged individualism was a noble characteristic of the nineteenth century . . . it scarcely fits into the twentieth."

The younger Big Five executives, including a few who had recently graduated from Harvard, were reasonably convinced that, within limits, employee morale was a sound business investment. They reasoned that if changes had to come it would be much better to bring them about voluntarily and retain control than to have some "rank outside labor leader" from the Pacific Coast force harsher measures upon them.

In accordance with the new line of reasoning, wage rates were increased in all occupations. Planned village communities were erected with small modern bungalows for employees. Fuel, medi-

Younger members of plantation communities are encouraged to learn plant grafting and all phases of scientific agriculture.

cal care and hospitalization were provided. Sums were spent for social halls, gymnasiums and athletic equipment. The Hawaiian Sugar Planters' Association, whose head had once compared laborers to jute bags, undertook a vigorous educational campaign to show their employees that malnutrition, through lack of a properly balanced diet, was seriously injuring their health and cutting down their working days. They were told what to do about it and helped to do it. Plantations set aside small areas for vegetable gardens and turned them over to the care of schoolboy sons of plantation employees. "Eat more green vegetables" became a plantation slogan.

By 1938 wages had risen to a daily average of $2.13, which the planters claimed compared favorably to the annual average for agricultural labor in the United States. Certainly labor had come a long way since the days when a half-dozen lashes from the Luna's (overseer's) black snake whip was considered the best solution to any labor difficulty, but it was not enough. Labor repeated that they wanted democracy, not paternalism. Their leaders demanded recognition of their own employee-controlled unions.

Labor was not the only threat to Big Five control. In the nineteen thirties, against the bitterest kind of opposition from the territorial quintet, outside capital began moving in. Sears Roebuck and Company, S. H. Kress and Company, The Piggly Wiggly Stores and a few other mainland concerns managed somehow to obtain sites. Their competitive prices were such a great relief and saving over the former one-price control that sales far exceeded their highest expectations and plans had to be made at once to expand and greatly increase their stocks.

In 1940 a C.I.O. Union won a National Labor Relations Board election and a signed contract for its sugar workers. This marked the beginning of a new era. It was the first time in the history of the sugar industry that employers had signed a union contract. In addition to their increasing labor trouble, a revolt appeared within the Big Five's own ranks.

World War II

In 1940 Army and Navy leaders were hurriedly preparing for war with Japan. In April of that year Rear Admiral Joseph Taussig told a Senate committee, "War with Japan is inevitable. Japan has already prepared her plan for crushing the United States."

Both branches of the services greatly strengthened their Hawaiian defense posts. Every conceivable type of defense maneuver was carried out. During a nine-day naval operation the nation was considered "at war with Japan" and one hundred and thirty warships, hundreds of planes, and forty-three thousand men steamed to the southwest from Pearl Harbor to execute a brilliant trial defense of Hawaii. Mock island invasions were staged. Oahu and the other islands were blacked out and a simulated enemy "sneak attack" from the air was quickly spotted and "defeated" by army spotlights.

By 1941 the Army had spent five hundred million dollars and the Navy two hundred and fifty million dollars in making Oahu into an "impregnable fortress," only to find out in less than an hour that, despite a half century of preparation and months of recent alerts against just such an eventuality, the much-vaunted bastion was not only pregnable but highly vulnerable to a surprise attack. In fifteen minutes Japanese bombers knocked out the Pacific Fleet and wiped out the entire air strength of Oahu. Many battleships, cruisers and destroyers were totally destroyed. American losses were staggering.

The sudden impact of the greatest defeat in American history plunged the "sugar-coated fortress" into a befuddled, feverish community.

Interracial suspicions flared. Eleven hundred suspects were singled out from the Territory's one hundred and fifty-nine thousand Japanese and placed under custody. There were charges and countercharges. There were also instances of "witch-hunting," where charges of disloyalty were used to pay off long-standing community grudges. Later it was conclusively proved and agreed by the War Department and by F.B.I. Chief J. Edgar Hoover that there was no sabotage of any type committed in the Islands at the time of the Pearl Harbor attack, immediately preceding that fateful day, or in the war years that followed.

Almost overnight the Big Five lost their political powers, ships, and consumer markets. Their sleek white luxury liners became dull gray troop ships. Several of their freighters were promptly sunk by submarines and the remainder taken over for military

Burning and damaged ships at Pearl Harbor on December 7, 1941.

supply vessels. As the defense industries absorbed nearly half of the plantation workers the sugar planters were forced to adopt a large mechanization program that reduced their employee requirements by more than twelve thousand men. Thousands of acres of plantation lands became airfields, housing projects, supply fields and military tent cities. All interisland communications were taken over.

The islands became Pacific War headquarters. Under the slogan "Remember Pearl Harbor" the people of Hawaii knuckled down to achieve a proud war record in America's darkest hour.

During the first few months the food situation was critical. Despite long-standing requests from the armed services, the planters had refused in previous years to convert part of their sugar lands to diversified farming, and as a result Hawaii was still importing ninety percent of its food supply. All food stocks were requisitioned and consumer prices were set by the authorities. Sugar and pineapples piled high on the docks. Shipments were uncertain. For a while the Big Five were forgotten by the man in the street as Hawaii changed from an agricultural to an industrial community for the first time in its history.

The decline of Big Five power continued during the war years. In the fall of 1942 a candidate who ran for the legislature on an anti-Big-Five campaign was swept into office with the second highest vote of any candidate. Early in 1943 Castle and Cooke, largest of the Big Five, were facing competition for the first time. In that year American Stevedores Ltd. was organized with independent capital. In the same year the Hawaiian Pineapple Company withdrew from the Pineapple Producers' Cooperative Association "because we have been advised by attorneys that the pooling contract is a violation of the Sherman Anti-Trust Act."

It was apparent that a new type of leadership was coming to the fore in the sugar and pineapple industries. It came somewhat as a shock to the kamaainas (old-timers) to read a statement from the new president of the largest sugar factor to the effect that he was not only willing but anxious to meet labor leaders in an effort to solve the new labor problems confronting the industry. The new industrialists were aware that there was going to be healthy competition in the postwar years and were streamlining their organizations accordingly. The multiple presidencies were gone and the interlocking directorates reduced. The Big Five was in the long, slow process of decentralization.

The emergence of new capital established a number of new business enterprises and strengthened the middle class. Islanders of small means pooled their resources together in syndicates known as huis. Hundreds of thousands of dollars were raised in this manner. Chinese, Japanese and people of mixed nationalities entered the entertainment field, established a new interisland airline, bought sugar plantations and cattle ranches, and went into the printing and publishing business.

The war was a great leveler and an important turning point in Hawaii's labor relations. "Labor missionaries" were sent out to the mills and plantations on every island to convert the sugar and pineapple workers. In the two years immediately following the end of military rule labor made greater gains than it had in the previous twenty years. The sudden influx of eighty-five thousand mainland workers, most of whom were unionized, gave impetus to the change. In a series of sweeping victories on Kauai, Hawaii and Maui plantations, a newly formed C.I.O. Union, using as its byword "Political Action—No Discrimination," won ninety-seven percent of the votes cast under the National Labor Relations Board.

In order to consolidate its gains labor became an articulate political force. In 1944 six of eight labor-endorsed senators were elected and sixteen of twenty-one labor-endorsed candidates won seats in the Territorial House of Representatives. Soon after the new legislature convened, a "Little Wagner Act" was passed, ex-

[123]

tending collective bargaining to all agricultural workers. A minimum wage law was set at forty cents per hour. Labor-endorsed legislation was introduced to ease the housing crisis among lower income families.

At the end of 1945 every sugar mill and cannery in Hawaii but one was organized under the powerful new C.I.O. Union. Under union rules all jobs were classified and each man paid according to the importance of his work. Jobs in the fields and canneries were rated according to education requirements, experience, manual skill, responsibility, initiative and judgment, physical effort, accident and health hazards, mental and visual attention required, and responsibility for the safety of others. By 1948 the union had called two major strikes and won millions of dollars in wage increases for its membership, which included practically all of the sugar, pineapple and dock workers.

Living conditions were greatly improved all over the Islands. The old plantation camps were on the way out. Model villages, modern in design as well as materials, were started on some plantations. New houses with three large bedrooms were built and made available to plantation families who formerly were crowded into small buildings.

It was amply evident that the social and economic gains brought about by World War II were not going to be relinquished for the former Big Five control. The mixed races had learned that they could improve their economic outlook only by organizing as one single body. No longer could they be used against each other. Nor could the disloyalty line be used to silence the Japanese; too many of them had won American, French and Italian citations for heroic devotion to the Allied cause. The old controls were no longer effective. Hawaii's agricultural workers had come up the ladder from peonage to democracy and were there to stay.

In 1946 the people of Hawaii were looking toward the future. After their all-out war effort they felt more closely united to the

United States than ever before. For the first time the banker, the tradesman and the plantation owner, the mill worker and the small business man saw the same thing and felt the same way about it. They agreed that there could be no real future for Hawaii without statehood.

All of the Territory's previous arguments for statehood were sound, especially the plea against further taxation without representation. But in 1946 there were a number of new reasons, two of which—racial loyalty and social progress—impressed far more people than all of the old figures on taxes paid, comparative land areas, or sugar and pineapple exports.

By virtue of its new labor laws the Territory rose to the front ranks in social legislation. Its workmen's compensation law was more liberal than the national average. Its child labor laws were strictly enforced. Its minimum wage and hour laws were more inclusive. Its unemployment compensation law assured more liberal benefits than such legislation in any other part of the United States with the possible exception of New York State.

There was no better proof of the surging ahead of democratic forces in Hawaii, or of the vast improvement in labor-management relations, than the fact that all classes joined forces on the statehood issue. This time all of the people wanted a voice and a vote on federal legislation; all wanted an assurance of preference against the cheaper Cuban sugar cane and against the downward revision of their quotas. Hawaii's political status provided a small measure of local government, with Washington holding the decisive power. This left the Hawaiian people without a representative in the Senate and with only one delegate in the House of Representatives—a delegate who could speak but was not allowed to vote. Hawaii had learned the hard way that a voteless territory was at the mercy of any and all types of discriminatory legislation.

During President Truman's message to Congress in 1946 he

urged "that Congress promptly accede to the wishes of the people of Hawaii that the Territory be admitted to Statehood in our Union." A Congressional investigating committee which had just returned from the Islands stated that "the United States by granting statehood to Hawaii could demonstrate to the world that it means what it says and practices what it urges when advocating true democracy for all peoples." In 1947 the House of Representatives approved statehood for Hawaii. A Gallup Poll revealed that mainland Americans favored statehood for Hawaii three to one. Who then was opposed to it?

According to former Secretary of the Interior Harold L. Ickes, the Navy was secretly blocking statehood through its effective Washington lobby. Senator Ellender of Louisiana, together with a number of other representatives from sugar states, added their opposition. A scattering of race-minded legislators repeatedly injected the issue of "white supremacy" under the guise of questioning Japanese-American loyalty and principles. "Can the Japanese in Hawaii really be trusted?" was one of the questions most frequently raised.

Late in 1943 the commander of a unit of Japanese-Americans from Hawaii, fighting in the mountains above the Gulf of Salerno, reported that his men charged into battle with "smiles on their faces" and added, "they feel they have something extra to fight for—it's a chance to prove they are real Americans."

The crack Japanese-American 100th Infantry Battalion spearheaded the Fifth Army advance, fought its way across the Volturno and Rapido rivers and led the break-through on Rome. These men were the first Americans to knock out a German tank in Italy. Because of heavy combat casualties they became known as the Purple Heart Battalion. The heroic "Go for Broke" (hold nothing back) spirit of the Japanese-American 442nd Regimental Combat Team repeatedly turned defeat into victory. In some of the bitterest fighting of the war the men advanced fifty miles in four days, often without food or sleep. As the spearhead of the spearhead of the Fifth Army they liberated eleven towns and villages, stormed and took two major objectives—and never took a backward step or lost a foot of ground they had won.

On the Benevento front, Sergeant Yutaka Nezu from Oahu led a squad into no man's land and rescued twenty-two American paratroopers who had been cut off behind the German lines for sixteen days. "Go for Broke" Japanese-Americans from Hawaii held the fierce Castle Hill sector against elite German counterattacking troops. They launched one of the first infantry attacks at Cassino.

Members of the 442nd Regimental Combat Team won eight presidential citations and more than a thousand Purple Hearts. By V-J Day the 100th, which became part of the 442nd Regiment, had achieved the heroic distinction of being the most decorated unit in the history of the United States Army.

Eighty-eight percent of Hawaii's war-wounded were of Japanese ancestry, and in village rolls honoring those who died in battle Japanese names outnumber all others. On the home front, Hawaii was the only state or territory to exceed every War Loan quota set in the first two years of war. Every racial group in the Islands made its own proud contribution to victory.

In 1959, on visiting Hawaii for the first time, several senators were visibly startled to see a number of races mingling together naturally and easily. They found that there is more real democracy and less racial prejudice and discrimination in Hawaii than in any other place in the United States. Two Southern senators, in particular, were greatly surprised to learn that racial intermarriage had increased to thirty-nine percent of the total. It was apparent that Jim-Crow laws and racial segregation would not be tolerated for one day anywhere in Hawaii.

As evidence of the Hawaiians' tolerance and respect for minority groups and their support of good leadership regardless of race,

[127]

the records show that a Negro was once elected to the Territorial House of Representatives from a district in which there were less than five hundred registered Negro voters.

Having long since come of age as a Territory, the people of Hawaii looked toward statehood as the fulfillment of their democratic ideals. They wanted to believe that President Franklin D. Roosevelt spoke for the nation when he declared that "Americanism is not and never was a matter of race or ancestry."

Chapter seven

STATEHOOD AND ITS RESOURCES

*P*EOPLE FROM ALL OF THE ISLANDS, INCLUDING SCHOOL CHILDREN, Boy and Girl Scouts and University students, helped assemble a petition for statehood that was six feet wide and a mile long and contained one hundred and sixteen thousand signatures. It was presented to the United States Senate in February, 1954. Some Hawaiians took up the cry of the American Revolution, "taxation without representation," for the blood of some of the Islanders traces back to the Boston Tea Party. But more than anything else they wanted to advance from second-class status to full citizenship.

Prejudice against statehood for Hawaii softened, but remained effective enough to keep the Islands a territory for fourteen post-war years. Each year the majority of negative votes came from a Southern bloc determined to avoid another "civil rights state." Charges of Communism were used as a smokescreen for racism and other issues. The strategy of delaying tactics, sidetracking and investigations was used. Every successful delay was followed by still another investigation. The records of investigations contain over three million words, equal to seventy-five books like this one.

The firm support of mainland people became increasingly apparent in 1958 among newspapers, civic groups, senators and representatives who were convinced Hawaii is America's most

[129]

impressive example of racial democracy in action. Victory in the long struggle came early in 1959. Congressional leaders gave their support and both chambers passed the Statehood Bill by wide margins.

The spontaneous jubilation that broke out on March 12, 1959, when the news reached the Islands, set off the greatest celebration in Hawaiian history. The Honolulu stock market skyrocketed, and it has been estimated that land values went up twenty percent. One of the young boys who dives for dimes and quarters off of Pier 14 was heard to shout, "Now I can be President!" An astronomy student told his classmates, "Now the sun will shine two hours longer on the U.S.A."

A rainbow glowed over Manao Valley and a fine misty rain fell on Honolulu the day statehood was approved. "Those beyond the clouds have sent their blessings," said the old Hawaiians. A Chinese mother said simply, "We now have the feeling of belonging." At night members of the 442nd's "Go for Broke" Regiment said a prayer at the National Memorial Cemetery of the Pacific in Punchbowl Crater. On that moonless night forty-nine torches lighted the graves of veterans from each state, and a fiftieth torch was for Hawaii and all its dead. Said Senator Daniel Inouye, a 442nd veteran, "We wanted to let the boys know we made it."

When the initial statehood enthusiasm subsided, Hawaiians found they were directly competing with forty-nine other states. There are many disadvantages to living on an island, especially when you are dependent on a mainland twenty-one hundred miles away for two-thirds of your necessities. Ships are to Hawaii what trains are to the mainland and everyone fears the possibility of a shipping strike.

Hawaii is no longer the low-cost producing area it once was, and a major problem for most people in 1960 was the high cost of living—about twenty-five percent higher than on the Pacific Coast. Hawaii's average income is slightly below the national average, but because of low taxes on land the taxes on Hawaiian income are among the highest in the world. As one kamaaina (old-timer) put it, "We need to attract new businesses and we need to produce more of our own needs. We have a young population and unless we provide more jobs for them they will go elsewhere and we will become an old community."

In recent years, in the search for new, diversified crops that will rival sugar and pineapples, several products have made big gains and shown unusual growth possibilities for the future.

Experiments conducted by the Department of Soils and Chemistry of the University of Hawaii have shown that a number of crops can be profitably grown on lava land that was once thought useless. Papaya, guava and passion fruit all grow well on lava land, as does acerola cherry, now being developed for its high Vitamin C content. In 1960 continuing experiments with tree crops were under way, with every indication that Hawaii's many miles of coarse black lava land might soon become an important new productive area.

When the University began experimenting with passion fruit in 1950 the fruit was practically unheard of commercially. Tests were so successful that many small farmers began planting part of their acreage in passion vines. The fruit, which matures in less than a year, is used for juice, for flavoring in ice cream, and as an ingredient of icings and cake fillings. It is expected that passion fruit production may someday become a major industry. Several companies on Oahu and one at Hilo process passion fruit, guava and papaya. Bulk juices are shipped to the mainland for processing into punches and blends. One company on Maui cans mangoes in syrup, and a small range of exotic fruit and nut foods are exported to the mainland.

Reclamation of lava lands for agricultural purposes has been

Macadamia nuts must be allowed to ripen until they fall naturally from the tree, and are harvested from the ground by hand.

notably successful in the macadamia nut industry. Against challenging odds, hundreds of acres of jungle-covered lava lands near Hilo have been converted into macadamia nut orchards.

Native to Australia, the macadamia produces a small, round, tasty nut with a flavor somewhere between an almond and a Brazil nut. It is grown in commercial quantities only in Hawaii. More than twenty years of patient selecting and grafting have produced superior varieties that outyield the old unimproved varieties as much as ten to one. Nothing is left to chance. Even

[132]

the selection of fertilizers is based on chemical research and on analysis of the leaves from macadamia trees.

The nuts are not ripe until they fall naturally from the trees and one of the big problems is to prevent them from falling into holes and crevices between the lava rocks. Vacuum-type mechanical harvesters, among other means, have been tried, but despite many experiments no mechanical device has yet proved as efficient as gathering the nuts by hand.

Hawaiian coffee, widely known for its aromatic flavor, is shipped direct from the Islands to such coffee centers as San Francisco, Tokyo, Manila, Antwerp and Genoa. The Island of Hawaii is the leader of diversified farming and its coffee production is concentrated chiefly in the Kona District because the soil there is loose and well drained and the temperature is ideal. In South America growers must plant other trees to shade the coffee bushes; at Kona the bushes get the beneficial early morning sun but are protected during the hottest parts of the day by an umbrella of daily clouds that reach out over the entire coffee-growing area. For this reason perhaps more than any other, Kona produces the only coffee grown commercially on United States soil.

Even in the best years most of the hundreds of small coffee farmers make no better than a fair living. A strong feeling for the land and for independence of a sort leads them to prefer the hard life of a coffee farmer to labor for someone else. Because the average returns are small, costs must be kept down and everybody helps during coffee picking time. Boys and girls of all ages go burrowing deep into the bushes to find the hidden berries and drop them into lauhala baskets.

The Japanese, who comprise most of the small growers, have developed with their own ingenuity and the aid of science an advanced method of coffee growing. Frequently they set new production-per-acre records. Nevertheless, in some years—despite

Coffee lands of the Huehue ranch at Kailua, on the Kona Coast of Hawaii.

the best efforts of Kona farmers—low prices, overproduction in
South America and marketing conditions beyond their control
have brought them low earnings and sometimes no earnings at all.
During the poorest years, when farmers have gone into debt, the
local government has extended assistance in the form of land tax
exemption.

In the extensive search for new crops cotton, wheat, rubber,
tobacco, silk and sisal have all been tried commercially but have
proved economically unsound. The growing of sandalwood, which
was once Hawaii's most valuable natural resource, has been at-
tempted recently but has met with little success. Some sandalwood

is found in remote areas on the high regions of Mauna Loa on Hawaii and in the heights of the Koolau Range on Oahu, but modern attempts to germinate seeds in nurseries have failed. It is estimated it would take more than a century for the sandalwood trees to develop the distinctive fragrance that made them so highly prized by Chinese mandarins as carved images and for sacred incense.

Millions of small distinctive Vanda orchids are shipped each month to the mainland and to cities around the world by the local floral industry. Of the thousands of varieties of orchids that grow well in the Islands commercial growers concentrate on three or four of the longest lasting and most popular types. Growers who specialize in plant sales produce over a thousand varieties to supply the needs of nurseries and orchid lovers everywhere. South Africa and Scandinavia are among the leading markets in Europe and Africa. Indonesia, Malaya and the Philippines receive frequent plant shipments, and the flowers are shipped regularly to a wide range of cities from Alaska to the Argentine.

The fragrance of such Hawaiian flowers as white ginger, carnations, plumiera, orchids, pikake and many others is distilled into an authentic Hawaiian perfume and a million-dollar, worldwide business. Each year the flower crops of many growers are contracted for and picked at the peak of their scent season. They are then distilled and are blended with certain chemicals, rare oils, ambergris, civit, rose attar and oil of sandalwood. Some of the essences cost over one thousand dollars a pint. Perfumes from Hawaii are even shipped to Paris, the perfume center of the world, and the market for the bottled fragrance of Island flowers is rapidly expanding.

Studies have shown that a profitable timber industry could be developed, especially on the Island of Hawaii. Among timber trees that grow well in the Islands are California redwood, Monterey pine, slash pine and loblolly pine, all softwoods. Among

[135]

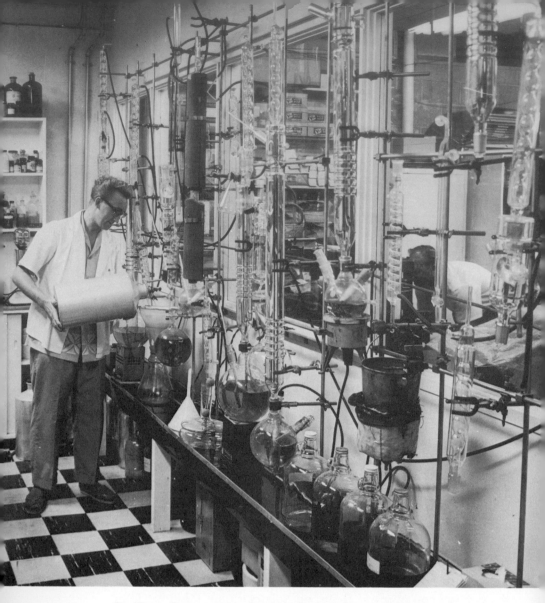

Dr. Horste Baumgaertner, chemist at Brown's Honolulu perfume factory, reduces oils extracted from Island flowers into essences for perfume.

the hardwoods are silver-gray Hawaiian ash, rose mahogany, lemon gum eucalyptus, and dark, rosy-tan cedar wood. Two mills on the Big Island are producing the native koa, ohia and monkeypod hardwoods for special uses in furniture and other items. A tree fern business on Hawaii is part of a growing industry that is based on something that nature created thousands of years ago in the primeval forests. One need only cut off the top of a giant fern tree, or a section, and place it in the ground, and it will root and continue to grow. Climbing vines, philodendron for example, twine around sections of tree fern and seem to thrive on it. Orchid growers have found that orchids will send their roots deep into tree fern and grow profusely. "Fernwood" products are now shipped all over the world.

Supplying taro for Island poi eaters is big business for many small farmers and processors. Most of the pastelike food is eaten in the Islands, but some is shipped to mainland cities where it is sold to former Islanders. Although imported rice and potatoes have reduced the demand for it, taro is still an important staple. "One-finger," "two-finger" or "three-finger" poi are the terms used to designate the consistency one prefers—for poi is almost always eaten with the fingers.

Water buffalo are still found to be more useful than tractors and less likely to get stuck in the mud working the underwater taro patches. Much of the former hand preparation has been taken over by processing plants that cook, wash, peel and grind the heavy roots into poi consistency and then pack it in neat bags. Now all the housewife has to do to the packaged poi she buys from a supermarket is to add water to obtain one-finger, two-finger or whatever gluey thickness her family prefers. New quick-freezing techniques provide frozen poi for Honolulu's frozen food counters. Recently taro processors have begun manufacturing and marketing taro flour for making taro bread. Macaroni and crackers have also been made from taro flour.

[137]

Sugar Cane

While Hawaii is working toward a more diversified agricultural era, sugar and the nearly as important pineapple remain the staple crops of the Fiftieth State, and its foremost industries.

Despite the boom in other activities, sugar is still king. It brings more money into the new state than the combined total of all the other Island products sent to the mainland, and employs more people than any other private enterprise. One out of every twelve employed people in the state receives his livelihood directly from sugar. This modern Island giant has been the mainstay of Hawaiian economy for over a hundred years.

Sugar, which provides six times as much nourishment for ten cents as bread, and twenty times as much as roast beef, is a carbohydrate food consisting of carbon, hydrogen and oxygen. The cane from which sugar is extracted is a grass with thick, tough stalks. The twenty steps in growing, harvesting and milling the cane into the refined white grains which we pour into our sugar bowls is a fascinating process.

The first step is the preparation of the soil by tractor subsoilers to a depth of two feet to permit young cane to send its roots down deep. Then large disc plows move in to smooth the earth and make it ready to receive the seed cane.

On all irrigated plantations surveyors must determine courses of cane rows and water ditches. Rows and ditches must closely follow the natural land contours, allowing not more than a two-percent grade, in order to prevent soil erosion. In some parts of the world oxen and crude plows are used to plant the cane, but in Hawaii this work is done by planting machines that make a furrow, drop a short piece of sugar cane stalk in, give it a squirt of fertilizer and cover the seed cane, all in one operation. Each stalk piece has buds, or "eyes," which soon sprout.

Then comes irrigation—one of the costliest steps in the production of sugar. The pumping plant for a large plantation is much larger than the one required by the city of Philadelphia. Most of the sugar cane grown on Maui, Oahu and Kauai depends largely upon a complex system of ditches, mountain tunnels and deep wells. This water supply system which supplies water to once arid and worthless land is one of the largest projects of its kind in the United States.

On the Island of Hawaii most of the plantations depend on the abundant rainfall of the northeastern Hamakua Coast to keep their cane lush and productive. Another distinctive feature on Hawaii is the small individual grower. In 1960 there were

Harvesting taro root from the underwater paddies of remote Waipio Valley on the Island of Hawaii.

Cane stalks are constantly inspected for maximum growth and productivity.

approximately twelve hundred independent farmers raising their own cane and having it milled by the Big Island sugar companies.

Up until the time that the cane is waist-high weeds are kept down by cultivators and mechanical sprays. All during the long growing season sugar scientists carefully watch the progress of the cane. They analyze plantation soils and prescribe like doctors for its requirements. Prescriptions are written in terms of phosphates, nitrates, potash or copper, which are supplied to the soil by special fertilizer machines. Air strips are maintained in some areas for aerial fertilizing.

Constant checks are made for insect pests and plant diseases. The long-range work of sugar scientists has practically eliminated all losses from such causes in Hawaii, but a constant "cane health" watch is maintained. Scientists also develop new canes. It takes six years, and loving care, to breed one new variety of cane.

Hawaiian sugar cane is allowed to grow from eighteen to twenty-four months before being harvested. Such a long growing season allows a maximum of sugar to form within the cane. As the sugar is formed it is stored in the form of a thin, sweet juice in the pithy stalk of the cane. As the cane nears maturity the sugar content of the juice increases. By harvest time the cane is fifteen to twenty feet high and ten percent by weight of the cane is sugar.

The cane fields are set on fire just before harvesting to destroy the trash and leaves that would hamper milling operations. Flames roar swiftly through the cane but do not harm the juice-filled stalks. After the big fires heavy push rakes or mechanical grabs break the stalks off at ground level and they are loaded by cranes for hauling to the mill. Hand cutting is still required on steep rainy slopes of unirrigated fields. Cane does not have to be replanted after the harvest, as the cane roots send up new plants. This growth is called a ratoon crop. From two to four ratoon crops are obtained from each planting of seed cane.

Hawaii's even climate makes it possible to schedule operations so that there is year-round activity in planting, cultivating, harvesting and milling. Each field is planted according to a carefully planned timetable that provides a continuous belt-line flow of cane into the mill. This practice means that the soil never rests; it is always producing or being cultivated, irrigated and fertilized according to needs. It also means steady employment and the establishment of permanent community homes in plantation areas —a unique feature of the Hawaiian sugar industry.

The mechanization of harvesting, which began during wartime manpower shortages, was given impetus by strikes and steadily rising wage levels until today the Island sugar industry is one of the most mechanized agricultural operations in the world. Hard physical field labor has been practically eliminated. Sugar workers in 1960 were receiving three times as much pay as formerly to produce the same yearly one million tons of sugar. Plantations are now accomplishing with seventeen thousand workers what it formerly took fifty-five thousand men to do.

The perishable harvested cane is rushed in heavy trucks to the mill, where it is unloaded into huge washing devices which remove dirt and trash. This material is returned to the fields to enrich the soil.

The first step in the milling process, which goes on twenty-four hours a day, is the squeezing of the juice out of the cane by passing it through a series of huge, high-pressure rollers. One hundred pounds of cane, in crushing, becomes one hundred and eight pounds of brown opaque juice and twenty-four pounds of bagasse. Bagasse, the waste material, is used for fuel to heat the factory boilers and is used for livestock feed and for the manufacture of paper by-products. Canec, a wallboard, is also made from the pithy, fibrous cane residue.

To prevent fermentation, a small amount of lime is added to the extracted juice, which then goes through heaters where the

[142]

Sugar cane ready for harvesting is set on fire to clean the stalks of leaves.

heat and lime start the clarifying process. In large settling tanks, called clarifiers, the hot lime slowly settles to the bottom, carrying impurities with it and leaving clear juice at the top. The clarified juice, straw-brown in color and translucent, is sent to evaporators and is brought to the boiling point by exhaust steam from mill engines. Vapor from the boiling juice of the first unit is used to boil the cane juice as it passes through a second evaporator. The vapor from the second unit boils the juice again as it passes through the third unit. Thus the same heat energy is used repeatedly.

[143]

After the evaporators have done their job of removing the water from it, the juice is a thick, amber-colored syrup. This syrup is still further evaporated in vacuum pans. As the water is boiled away from the syrup, crystals of raw sugar take form and grow in size. In the final process the crystals are separated from the syrup by the spinning action of centrifugal baskets, the screen of which retains the crystals but throws off the syrup. From one hundred pounds of cane twelve pounds of raw sugar is obtained and three pounds of molasses. The molasses is used for stock feed and fertilizer, and in the manufacture of alcohol.

Nearly all of the raw sugar produced in Hawaii is sent to the mainland in bulk form to be refined. Fast freighters carrying raw sugar and pineapples from Hawaii to the Pacific Coast now make the trip in less than a week. On the return trip they carry food, clothing, lumber, building supplies and many other things.

Oahu, which is the least productive of the four sugar islands, is the most important because it is the nerve center for the whole industry. The main offices and the Experiment Station are all in Honolulu and it is there that the main decisions and transactions are made. Two million dollars a year is spent on research by the planters' Experiment Station, the world's foremost sugar research center.

It is owing in no small part to the efforts of sugar scientists that Hawaii's plantations now produce more calories per acre than man has ever before extracted from the earth. From an area only eighteen miles square, barely larger than the area of New York City, Hawaii produces one-fourth of all the sugar manufactured under the American flag.

Hawaii's average sugar yield per acre in 1957 was 10.16 tons. The average for other sugar areas was: Louisiana, 1.76 tons per acre; Florida, 4.18 tons; Argentina, 1.06; Australia, 3.63; and Cuba, 2.09. These figures point up the vast differences in Hawaii's methods, climate, and soil compared with the rest of the world.

Today's sugar plantation is a complete community in itself existing under unusual conditions. The plantation worker makes his home where his job is, in one of the clean, modern little towns that have grown up in the sugar fields on each of the twenty-seven large plantations. Many employees rent their homes, but a growing number of plantations are selling land sites so that employees may build and own their own homes outright. Each plantation community has its own schools, hospitals, stores, churches, theatres, community buildings, playgrounds and recreation fields.

Pineapples

The pineapple industry, which began in a Honolulu barn and was thought of as an unique and exotic enterprise, now has the world's largest cannery and provides seventy percent of the world's pineapples. There are people in the Islands who can look back and recall the first small pineapple plantation; yet today in Hawaii pineapples are so much a part of modern Island life that nearly everyone in the Fiftieth State is affected by them.

During the time of the Gold Rush in California small pineapples were growing wild on the hillsides of Kona on the Big Island, but they were fibrous and sour. An English settler, Captain John Kidwell, found a bigger, juicier and sweeter variety growing in Jamaica. The captain imported one thousand slips of this better pineapple plant called the Smooth Cayenne, and it has since become the variety most commonly grown in Hawaii.

The pineapple is in many ways a wonder fruit. It is not grown from seeds. Very few cultivated pineapples have seeds, which is fortunate, because seeds when they do appear spread all through the pineapple and spoil it for eating or canning. Plants are grown from slips near the base of the fruit or from the crown at the top of a pineapple. When fully grown, the plant is three and a half to four feet tall and has over a hundred long, spiny leaves attached to a central stem.

The first signs of fruiting in a pineapple plant is the appearance of a red bud in the growing center about the size of a walnut. It is actually a miniature pineapple with approximately one hundred and fifty individual flowers, each of which eventually becomes an "eye" of the ripe fruit.

About fifteen months after planting, the miniature pineapple has reached a length of two or three inches and the individual flowers begin to blossom from the bottom up. The petals are pale blue and each flower blooms only for one day. After the petals wither and fall the center parts of the flowers remain and continue to grow. About twenty months after planting time the "golden fruit" is ready for harvest. It is solid and now weighs about five pounds.

Soon after the first crop is harvested preparations are made for the second or "ratoon" crop. The original stem can fruit no more but each of the suckers will produce a ripe pineapple the following year. After that the plants are usually knocked down and the fields prepared for new plantings. Sometimes the plants are allowed to make a second ratoon crop. The second ratoon pineapples issue from suckers which grow out of the first ratoon stumps.

Pineapple fields, like sugar fields, must be constantly cared for and supplied with the right plant nutrients. Soil preparation begins six to eight months before planting. The fields are plowed and harrowed until the soil surface is entirely broken up and all the vegetation that had been growing on it is mixed in. The process is repeated several times. Between plowings the earth is left to rest, soak in rainfall and decompose the plowed-in vegetation. At the time of the final plowing the soil is fumigated by injecting a chemical called D.D. six to eight inches deep in the topsoil. This chemical kills nematodes which could otherwise destroy the root systems of pineapple plants.

Some fields are planted in wide, graceful curves. This "contour planting" is done to provide easy, controlled drainage and prevent fast "run-offs" that might cause soil erosion. Other patterns are used depending usually upon the grade or slope of the fields. These various patterns help to divide the fields into working units and answer the requirements of the complicated plantation machines.

"Pines," as they are called by the people who work among them daily, are planted in the fall or spring depending on soil and weather conditions. Before the slips are planted, wide strips of mulch paper are laid entirely across the fields, forming long paper rows. This helps to prevent the growth of weeds, conserves moisture and fertilizer and increases soil temperature. The paper, simi-

Pineapple fields are terraced and contour-planted as a soil conservation project to combat erosion.

lar in appearance to light roofing paper, is unrolled by a machine
with two discs which cover both edges of the paper with soil to
hold it down. The paper is marked at the proper distances to show
planters the spots through which the slips are to be planted.

The planters begin as soon as slips have been distributed along
the sides. Each planter carries a narrow steel trowel which he
plunges through the mulch paper at the marked plant holes. A
hole is made with a quick twist of the planter's wrist. A slip is
thrust in with his other hand and he withdraws the trowel in a
skilled manner that lets the soil pack naturally around the plant.
To allow room for growth, no two plants in the same bed are set
out opposite each other. Nearly two thousand slips are planted
to the acre.

Weeds growing between the paper rows are removed to prevent them from absorbing water and nourishment needed by the
"pine" plants. Many men who once used hand hoes for this job
have been supplanted by one man who comes chugging along
with a mechanical cultivator. Chemical weed sprays are also used.

Plant development is closely studied by regular growth checks
and a monthly plant-to-plant crop log is maintained. As soon as
plants consume the plant foods in the soil new nutrient elements
must be added. The plant food most used by pineapples is nitrogen. Potassium and phosphorus may also be needed in varying
amounts. Nitrogen, potassium and phosphorus are applied me-
chanically near the base of the plant in the form of dry commercial
fertilizers. Iron, which is essential to the growth and development
of pineapples, is sprayed in solution form directly onto the leaves
of the plants as frequently as required during the growing period.
Sometimes zinc solutions are also used.

On the big islands most pineapple lands are located in the plateau areas and for the most part are not irrigated. On Lanai, the
"Pineapple Island"—a once arid wasteland—a large irrigation
system is used to supplement rainfall when needed. The world's

largest garden hose carries water from pipes to the nozzles of two tractor-mounted fifty-foot booms that travel around and machine-water twelve acres of pineapples every eight hours.

Cultivated pineapple plants are not rugged. If great care is not exercised to protect them against their enemies they will wilt and die, or else bear a sickly fruit that is unfit to eat. One of the "pines' " most persistent enemies is the many-legged white mealy bug which looks like a miniature powder puff. Despite its many legs, it never seems to want to use them very much. When it finds a comfortable spot it settles down and feeds on the juice in the plant leaves. In feeding it injects a toxic substance into the plant which damages and can kill the plant.

Ants are very fond of mealy bugs and carry them from place to place so that they can feed on the best pineapple leaves. The ants in turn "milk" the mealy bugs, which secrete a sticky substance that the ants relish. Finally the ants kill and eat the mealy bugs, but by then the bugs have severely damaged the plants.

For a long time vast pineapple fields were wilting and dying without any apparent reason. Many weeks before the plants began to wilt from the mealy bugs' toxic injections the ants herded their "cows" away to new pastures. When planters inspected the plants there was nothing to be seen other than what appeared to be a disease. Mealy bugs were rarely found on sick plants. If found at all, they were usually on healthy plants, and so for many months they were not thought to be the cause of "wilt disease." Eventually they were found to be the culprits and some new organic insecticides were developed to destroy them. Now an alert watch is maintained for "mealies" and as soon as they are spotted Malathion and other sprays are applied by a boom machine that reaches to the middle of the fields from both sides.

The continual work of a group of scientists and technicians at the Pineapple Research Institute is seldom heard of by the pineapple workers or by most Islanders; yet without their quiet work the pineapple industry could never have survived in the face of diseases, pests, weeds and soil deficiencies. The Pineapple Institute is an agricultural research organization devoted solely to pineapples and, like the sugar institute, is maintained without government support. Nine pineapple companies contribute jointly more than a million dollars yearly toward its scientific studies and research.

Some Island scientists specialize in soil tests, some concentrate on plant growth processes, and some study the effects of fertilizers and trace elements. The use of the chemical DDT as a soil fumigant was developed by Pineapple Research Institute scientists. After being patented it was made available for public use throughout the United States.

During the peak day and night harvesting season, mechanical boom harvesters offer a strange sight at night in the pineapple fields, with their huge spotlights and extended boomlights swaying in the air. Trained pickers walk along the rows selecting the fully ripe fruit. They snap the pineapples from the stalks, strike off the crowns and place them on the long narrow conveyor belt extending far out on a boom from the harvester. When the fruit reaches the harvester it is conveyed to the top and then rolls into a big bin. After the bin is full the harvester is raised up, allowing the truck with the full bin to drive away while an empty one takes its place.

At the cannery the hearts of the pineapples are cut into cylinders or chunks and canned. The leftover shells, ends and trimmings are shredded and dehydrated to produce millions of pounds of pineapple bran for livestock feed. "Mill juice" pressed from the same material is processed to recover citric acid, which is used in the manufacture of drugs, soft drinks and foods. Recaptured mill juice is also processed and converted into natural sugar syrup and used in canning the fruit. Because of its progressive field and cannery methods Hawaii now outstrips all other areas of the world combined in the production of pineapple products.

Harvester crews place fruit on conveyor which carries it in to the bins while the truck moves slowly ahead.

Other Island State Products

Aside from pineapples Hawaii has a wide range of semitropical fruits. Many Islanders have mangoes, bananas, lilikoi (passion fruit), avocados, coconuts, papaya and other fruits growing in their backyards. Yellow guavas and berries still grow wild in some of the forested hillsides. Bananas, which came to Hawaii with the

[151]

early migrations, remain one of the most widely used Island foods. Cooking bananas, which take the place of potatoes in some homes, are frequently served up with curry, fish or other typical Island dishes.

The papaya is Hawaii's most popular breakfast fruit and Islanders are quick to point out that a papaya for breakfast contains far more Vitamin A and eighty times as much Vitamin C as one orange. The papaya, which resembles a small melon, is frequently eaten with a few drops of lemon juice for breakfast, or is used for dessert mixed in fruit cocktail. It is also used in jam alone or with other fruits.

The mango, an ancient fruit from India that was introduced to Hawaii from the Philippines, is the most exotic of the Island State's agricultural products. A mango resembles a juicy peach more than any other fruit, but its skin is smoother, its shape is longer and it has a fibrous central pit. Considered by many to be the best-tasting fruit in the world, mangoes are best eaten fresh. They also may be made into pies or canned like peaches.

Although many people think of Hawaii in connection with pineapples, sugar cane and fruit, actually the raising of beef cattle was established as a major industry long before sugar and today holds a substantially increasing place in the new state's economy.

Island cowboys were riding the windswept Hawaiian ranges for many years before Texan "cowpokes" began driving their longhorn steers to market along the old Chisholm trail. King Kamehameha owned all the original herds. But after the Great Mahele (division of land) selected herds were settled on private ranches, including the huge Parker range.

The Hawaiians learned to ride and rope and break broncos from fast-riding Spanish vaqueros who were brought over from Mexico with their red bandanas, ponchos, broad-winged stirrups, black and white hand-twisted hair-rope and four-strand hand-braided lassos.

[152]

Native Hawaiians loved the wild-riding life of an Island cowboy and became outstanding paniolas (Hawaiian cowboys) in their own right. They learned that the lasso as handled by the tough bronco-riding vaqueros was a more formidable weapon than a rifle or a revolver.

The Hawaiian paniola became as skillful, as reckless and as hard-riding as the Spaniards from whom he took the name. He came to know that a cowboy's friends are his rope and his horse. In Wyoming one year Hawaii's Ikua Purdy won the world's steer roping championship with two other Hawaiians taking third and sixth place. Eben Low, grandson of the founder of the Parker Ranch, was another world-famed cowboy. Even after he lost one hand in a roping accident Low challenged any man to top his roping skill. At Cheyenne, Wyoming, "Rawhide Ben," as Low was called, was crowned the one-handed champion roper of the world.

Of the Fiftieth State's four million total acres of land, about one-fourth, or one million acres, is given over to cattle ranching. Most of these ranches are located above the sugar and pineapple fields and below the forest reserves. Improved English breeds of Hereford, Shorthorn and Aberdeen Angus were brought in, but Hereford became most popular and today over ninety percent of the state's beef cattle are Herefords.

Much progress has been made in improving the cattle by planting better and more nutritious grass, by rotational grazing and by new ranch management methods. As the Islands do not produce the typical steer-fattening feed, such as corn, cattlemen have turned to the use of molasses to help fatten their Island beef. The wild, racy longhorn steer that roamed the range in Kamehameha's day has been replaced by a sleek, fat, sugar-fed cousin who prefers to forage in the molasses bin.

Hawaii was once thought to be completely lacking in mineral resources, but recently several forms of mineral wealth have been discovered. Only three years ago rich bauxite deposits were found on Kauai and on the Island of Hawaii. The aluminum-rich ore

[153]

Hawaiian cowboys in gay spirits after a day's roundup on the Waimea range.

deposits are estimated to be larger than any known deposit in the United States, which imports eighty-two percent of its aluminum bauxite supply. Most of the major United States aluminum companies are investigating the possibilities of the Hawaiian deposits.

Reef limestone has been quarried for use as building material, and lava rock is now being used also as an Island building material. The latter is becoming increasingly popular for its decorative value in gardens, walls and buildings because its rough natural finish blends well with Island landscaping. Its strengthening qualities and resistance to corrosion have made it of use as a glaze for tile pipes.

There are other possible uses for the coarse, black commonest rock found in Hawaii. In Italy a method has been developed for making fiber and other material from lava rock. It is considered possible that in another twenty years Islanders may be wearing dresses or suits of clothes made from the rocks that were once thought useless.

The sea that surrounds Hawaii is also considered a part of the state's natural resources. The Islands are located on the edge of the richest faunal area in the world, and the ocean floor drops sharply from shallow reef-bound inshore areas to great ocean depths. Vast fish resources are to be found in all directions. To the south there are tremendous quantities of prized yellow-fin tuna. To the north are large areas for albacore, the species of tuna that is considered the best for canning purposes. Large quantities of aku (tuna) are taken from the waters close to the islands. Aku, because of their high quality as a canned food, have become the major product of the state's largest single fishery.

The biggest problem of Hawaiian commercial fishermen has always been the lack of a large supply of live bait. A small silvery anchovy that is ordinarily used is too fragile and easily injured in the live bait well of a boat that is rolling about in the heavy seas off Hawaii. Scientists of the U. S. Fish and Wildlife Service have been trying to develop methods of fishing that do not require the use of live bait. One method that is currently being investigated is that of electro fishing in which an electric current is used to force the fish to swim to the boat where they may be easily caught. Many sporting people and conservation groups oppose this method.

Japanese sampans, first brought to Hawaii from the Orient many decades ago, are still considered the best boats for the

[155]

Sampan fishermen from Kewalo Basin strike a run of tuna off Oahu.

choppy, sometimes heavy-thrusting seas off Hawaii. Long before dawn the fleets of rakish kewalo-blue sampans leave their harbors. Once they are clear of land a lookout watches sharply for groups of circling birds—a sure sign that fish are about. When circles of diving, raucous-screaming birds are located the fishermen line the broad sterns of their sampans and, casting out, soon have a steady stream of fish hitting the decks. Lines are quickly

[156]

cast out again and again until the wide-ranging school of aku shears off and disappears.

Sampan skippers continue the search for tuna throughout the day and usually remain offshore until they have made a good catch or their supply of live bait runs out. Aku sampans often come in with a ton or more of fish aboard and occasionally catch as much as forty thousand pounds in one day. Big black marlin have been caught that weighed over two thousand pounds. They also catch the swift ono and mahimahi (dolphin), the fish that gourmets love. Mahimahi, which tastes like halibut but is not as dry, is the fish most often seen on Island restaurant menus. Bottom fishing for snappers takes place in from forty to one hundred and sixty fathoms of water. Along reef and inshore areas large quantities of smaller fish are taken for the local markets. Mullet, uloa (African pompano), oio (bonefish), kaku (barracuda), lobsters, puhi (eels), hee (octopus) and other sea foods are much in demand.

Besides the yearly threat of typhoons, every fisherman and every coastal dweller in the state is aware that one of Hawaii's most destructive dangers is the tidal wave. A new Island warning system, now in effect, is the result of much loss of life and property damage from tidal waves during the past fifteen years.

When an earthquake occurs off Japan or the Aleutians huge amounts of sea water are dislocated by a depression in the ocean. The rush of water to fill the void results in a broad, three hundred to six hundred mile per hour sea wave. When such a wave approaches a land mass like Hawaii it sometimes builds up to great heights and crashes over the coastline, destroying everything before it.

When the great, roaring tidal wave of 1946 hit Hawaii it left one hundred and fifty-nine people dead and twenty-five million dollars worth of damage. Another in 1952 created havoc and did much damage. The big tidal wave of 1957 took two lives and cost three million dollars in property damage.

Scientists cannot predict with positive accuracy what a tidal

[157]

wave will do or where it will die out. But modern seismographic equipment can tell when an underwater earthquake starts a wave and it can tell where the wave is going.

After the 1957 disaster, Islanders demanded an effective warning system. In 1960 the Honolulu Magnetic and Seismological Observatory, a nerve center for tracking seismic waves, will be in operation at Ewa Beach and will serve as the center of a seawave warning system covering two-thirds of the Pacific Ocean. From its amazingly delicate magnetic equipment will come the first word of any tidal wave aimed at Hawaii.

Under the new warning system in use today, civil defense officials set off twenty-three powerful coastal sirens. At the same time police cars, fire-fighting equipment and helicopters rush to the seashores to warn everyone away and evacuate coastal residents to ground that is at least fifty feet above sea level.

Chapter eight

FUTURE OF THE FIFTIETH STATE

Land and Homes

$\mathcal{T}$HERE WAS ONCE A TIME IN HAWAII WHEN IF YOU WANTED A home you simply picked a likely spot, cleared it a little, tied some frame poles together and covered it with tough pili grass. If a storm blew it down you took a day off from fishing and easily put up another. But like the old gray mare the little grass shack is long past in modern Hawaii.

Today if you want a home on Oahu you begin by forgetting all about Waikiki and start looking for a site in suburban areas twelve miles from Honolulu. A choice lot with a view will cost about $2.50 per square foot or about $110,000 an acre. Really choice land close to the city was selling in 1960 at more than a million dollars an acre.

In 1959 the state's twelve largest landowners owned fifty-three percent of all private lands. The largest single owner, Bishop estate, was a royal holding; others were acquired by purchase or gift. Richard Smart, owner of the 187,000 acre Parker Ranch, is the second largest private landowner and the Damon estate, whose founder was the son of a missionary, is the third largest.

The Bernice P. Bishop estate, which controls about eight percent of the total land area, traces directly back to the Great Mahele or land division of the eighteen forties and eighteen fifties.

The Great Mahele and the Bill of Rights, sometimes called

[159]

Hawaii's Magna Carta, were the beginning of private land rights. During the Mahele the king, who had previously owned all the land, divided it among the chiefs, the government, the common people and himself.

Much of the land soon passed into the hands of non-Hawaiians, by sale, lease, or marriage. Less than fifty years after the great division fifty-seven percent of the taxable land belonged to sugar planters, cattle ranchers and a few others. Today in addition to the twelve huge private holdings the state and other government agencies hold more than forty-two percent of all land. The most valuable public land is held by the Armed Forces.

So much land is in the hands of a few people who decline to sell that small farmers in diversified agriculture often must be satisfied with short leases. Sometimes the leases are oral and only for one year. Lessees seldom get any credit for improvements they make on leased agricultural lands. Like land, most of the water resources are controlled by large landowners. Irrigation on the large islands is directed primarily by sugar and pineapple interests or private companies closely connected with the sugar industry. The small farmer therefore must depend largely on rainfall and marginal land.

A large number of homesteading plans have been carried out for the purpose of getting Hawaiians and part-Hawaiians out of the congested slum areas and onto small farms. The plan, at first confined to Molokai, has been extended to other islands. Very few of the homestead-supporting farms have been successful for a number of reasons, but mainly because agriculture is geared to large-scale operations and because most homesteaders were city-accustomed people unable to readjust easily to difficult farming conditions. Small residential and subsistence homesteads in the vicinity of towns where the Hawaiians have employment have worked out much better. The plan as a whole has done a lot of good but has fallen far short of the goals envisioned by its founders.

In 1959 almost twenty thousand acres of federal and state lands were slated to be turned over to Islanders for industrial, farm and residential use. The Hawaiian legislature approved a plan to open up seven thousand acres of state-owned lands in the Waimanalo Valley on Oahu and nine thousand acres at Kamuela on the Big Island. The first step called for a model farm subdivision, with each plot area large enough for a family to make a living from its cultivation. The United States Congress authorized a program to aid property owners and farmers on the Big Island by allowing them to exchange land damaged in the 1955 volcanic eruption for state lands.

In 1959 Governor William F. Quinn sent a plan to the legislature calling for a second Mahele for agriculture. The measure called for opening up ten-acre farm plots to farmers dispossessed by urban growth on Oahu. Resale of the land would be prohibited for many years. An important feature of the measure was its proposal to sell the ten-acre plots by drawing lots instead of by public auction, in order to prevent speculation.

In 1960 shacks, firetraps and large slum areas that have always been a blot on downtown Honolulu were in the process of having their faces lifted by a thirty-million-dollar redevelopment plan. The first five years of statehood will see over two hundred acres of blighted city slums wiped out and replaced by modern residential and business areas.

As for Waikiki, a business and industrial boom has completely changed its skyline. Its spectacular new steel and concrete Ala Moana business center houses eighty stores surrounded by double-deck parking for seven thousand cars. A fabulous new restaurant atop a fourteen story building will revolve once every hour so that diners can enjoy changing views of mountain and sea.

All of the land in the large Waikiki area soon will be used for multiple family dwellings and co-op apartments. Property has become so valuable that many Waikiki people can't afford to live

[161]

Twenty-eight million dollar Ala Moana Shopping Center opened late in 1959.

in their small houses any more. The trend is toward consolidation. People with five thousand square feet of land join another family or other neighbors in the same fix and form a hui (company) so that they can erect a bigger building to house more people in the same area. Honolulu has long had a higher population density than Japan or England and people in Waikiki and other crowded areas have learned to live closely with the least noise and disturbance.

The ringing hammers of Honolulu's building boom grow louder not only in town but all over the state. A combination of fast-growing population and an increasing economy has increased the pressure of people seeking new homes. What once were the quiet little suburbs of Honolulu are not so quiet now. The booming population of Windward Oahu has nearly doubled in less than ten years.

Hawaii has long pioneered in an indoor-outdoor type of living that combines the charm and simplicity of Oriental with Polynesian features. The straight, stiff lines and small, high windows of New England missionary houses have been replaced by an informal, open way of living that takes full advantage of the mild year-round climate. This type of architecture, called "contemporary Hawaiian," is strongly influenced by the mixtures of races and cultures in the Islands.

Many houses have high-beamed ceilings which, combined with

Modern Hawaiian home with open lanai and tropical garden.

good cross ventilation, provide comfort without air conditioning. The lanai, a porch or terrace, brings outdoor vistas into the house and makes family living the most informal possible. Usually covered to provide shade and protection from the rain, the lanai is used as a sort of outdoor living room where much of the entertaining is done. For seats, houses usually have punees (couches) or zabutons (floor cushions) on the lanai.

Many houses have sliding shoji doors, tatami mats for the floor and a tokonoma—an alcove for flowers. Such materials as lava rock, Waianae sandstone, bamboo and sisal, as well as Island carvings, murals and tropical tile make Island houses definitely Hawaiian in appearance and feeling.

Growth and progress has not lessened the warm friendliness of Hawaii. Most people are busy but never in too much of a hurry for graciousness. If you go to visit a Hawaiian at his home you will be greeted with "Hele mai; nou ka hale"—"Come on in; the house is yours"—for aloha still means friendship and hospitality as well as welcome or farewell.

Youth and Achievements

Each year in Honolulu produces a larger number of fifteen-year-old and nineteen-year-old corporation presidents, vice presidents and young assistants by the hundreds, manufacturing and selling products of their own design and construction. Some of the youthful enterprises are so successful in creating things people need that their production managers have a hard time keeping up with sales.

When most boys and girls in the United States get their first job after school, on weekends or during vacation, they get paid for their services usually without knowing where the money comes from or how. Such terms as net earnings and dividends have only vague meanings. In Hawaii, however, a large number of young

[164]

Young Hawaiians are serious students. An increasing number are taking vocational training to meet the demand for skilled craftsmen.

people learn the answers to such questions in their own private businesses called "Junior Achievement companies." They experience the satisfactions of a business venture, the hard work that precedes success, and sometimes the disappointment of a failure.

The Junior Achievement program, which has over sixty thousand members on the mainland, was introduced to the young people of Hawaii in 1958 by Earl J. Goris with the firm support of Police Chief Dan Lui and many business leaders. The purpose of the program is to provide teen-agers with firsthand experience in business and the opportunity to find out how products and profits are made.

In the course of a school year Hawaii's Junior Achievers go through the complete cycle of founding, operating and closing out a real business. They organize companies, elect officers and directors, manufacture and sell merchandise of many kinds, study production and personnel problems and hold annual meetings.

In conformity with the national program they organize their businesses in September, get into full production in October and November and take advantage of Christmas season sales to declare a dividend if possible.

Each separate Junior Achievement company must finance itself through the sale of stock and the production and sale of products or services. Stock is fifty cents a share and no one individual may own more than five shares. Supplementary assistance is provided by public-spirited firms, who provide each young company they sponsor with the services of three supervisors and take care of administrative and other expenses.

Products and services provided by Hawaii's teen-age business people include a wide range of things. Jaboh (Junior Achievement Bank of Hawaii) sponsored by the Bank of Hawaii, operates a bank for Junior Achievers, handles loans and provides many other banking services. Other junior companies produce and sell home lubricants, bundles of kindling wood, barbecue fire starters, aromatic candles, walking stilts, wax goods and other items. One teen-age company calling itself the C and C Associates buys, packs and distributes food items in an attractive Hawaiian gift box. A youthful service contract company contracts to sell refreshments at public meetings.

Just as the presidents of sugar and pineapple companies have a central location for major decisions, the teen-age JA executives make the Honolulu Armory their center for research, production

1959 Waikiki Skyline showing latest developments, with Diamond Head Crater and part of windward Oahu in the background.

facilities, banking, office quarters and administrative headquarters. So successful was the program in its first year that production more than doubled in 1959. The enterprising Junior Achievers who play such a progressive part in Hawaiian life today may well look toward a future bright with aloha.

The real romance of Hawaii in 1960 is not coco palms, hula girls or tropical sunsets. It is the romance of reality, the bright and challenging prospects of the future. Statehood and jet travel have already brought tremendous changes. Commerce is increasing. Great new buildings are under way. Land is being developed and resorts to rival Waikiki will be established on the outer islands.

Because of the youthfulness of the population, forty-three percent of whom are under nineteen years of age, the state must develop more than five thousand new jobs each year. One of the outstanding possibilities is the creation of a large paper industry based on bagasse. Continued experimentation in tropical fruits, flowers and by-products goes on in the hope that another crop will be developed to rank beside pineapples and sugar. In 1960 Hawaii's fast-growing textile industry was setting tropical garment fashions for the nation. The Islands' first steel mill was put in operation in 1959 and a forty million dollar oil refinery was under construction. Within the memory of those living Hawaii has become an industrialized modern community.

Island Space Stations

The Fiftieth State and its wind-swept, isolated satellite tracking stations play a vital role in the movement of mankind toward outer space.

Geophysical scientists consider Hawaii one of the most important spots on earth from which to view the stars and planets. All the important stars are visible from the dust and smog-free mountain tops. The Southern Cross and the two first magnitude stars Alpha and Beta Centauri that are conspicuous in Hawaii's summer sky are not visible to advantage from any other part of the United States.

With Hawaii playing an important part in space probing, Island boys are keen to learn all about objects to be seen in the sky. To meet this interest Bishop Museum has developed a program of simple astronomy and in 1959 completed a planetarium and small observatory.

The geophysical nature of Hawaii (its location in the center of the Pacific close to the equator) makes it extremely important as a point for tracking rockets and satellites. Its four separate facilities for tracking space satellites, communicating with them and observing them are vital to the nation's space program.

The Ka-Lae (meaning clear or calm) Field Space Laboratory at South Point on the southernmost tip of the Big Island is the most important tracking station in the world. Electronic devices at South Point can contact a whirling satellite thousands of miles in outer space.

The latest advance in space-age communications is an eighty-four foot radio telescope atop a building at the Navy's Radio Station in Wahiawa that bounces high-frequency impulses off the moon directly to Washington. From Hawaii signals are not hampered by the earth's curvature, which is the drawback in many other global locations. The Navy expects to achieve a range of five thousand miles by using the moon as a passive relay.

An observatory to track man-made satellites and photograph them with great precision against a background of stars has been erected on the high, clear summits of Haleakala, Maui, by the Smithsonian Institution. The ten thousand foot high station tops eleven others scattered around the earth in terms of clear atmosphere and weather conditions favorable to celestial observations.

Haleakala's "big eye," a six thousand pound Baker-Nunn camera, can film a satellite two thousand miles away in space. The camera works with a precision of one ten thousandth of an inch and its twenty-inch lens can photograph an apple or a potato five hundred miles away.

Jet Era

The long-awaited Pacific jet age arrived in Hawaii in 1959 with jets swooping down on Honolulu's International Airport from all parts of the mainland and the Pacific. What was once a six months' voyage by sail from Hawaii to Boston has become a matter of only nine and a half hours' flying time.

Jets also became the big news in Hawaiian interisland transportation. With the new state already having more airports than seaports, its new jet interisland "air buses" make it a simple matter to commute between islands. It now takes no more time to get from the other islands to Honolulu by air than it does for Chicago or New York commuters to get to work from their suburban homes.

Honolulu's new twenty-four million dollar jet-age air terminal is scheduled for completion early in 1961. No other archipelago in the world has advanced from early primitive to jet-age modern in so short a time.

Twenty years ago a prediction of a regularly scheduled four-and-a-half-hour flight in the near future between Hawaii and the Pacific Coast would have been regarded as a wild statement. Yet, in a few years more it will be as commonplace to go from the Pacific Coast to Hawaii for the weekend as to go for an overnight visit into the country.

Already in the planning stage is a plane that will shatter the time barrier and reduce flying time between New York and Honolulu to three hours. It is expected to be in operation by 1970. With another plane, a Lockheed supersonic slated for 1967 delivery, Honolulu will be only one hour and forty-five minutes away from San Francisco. Considering the two hours' difference in time between the two cities you may then finish one breakfast in San Francisco at 8:00 A.M. and gain enough time flying across the Pacific to arrive at Honolulu for a second breakfast at 8:00 A.M. Hawaii time.

Atomic-powered ships may greatly reduce the sea time to Hawaii within the next ten years and an international free port may develop at Honolulu to admit foreign raw material for local manufacture and to help the Islands compete in the complex economy of today and tomorrow. It is certain that the state that was once a kingdom will be the center of a new Pacific Age whose culture will be a unique blending of East and West.

The shrinking of the world through jet air travel makes possible a more direct and personal exchange of ideas between people. The dean of the University of Hawaii envisions for the Fiftieth State an Institute of Mental Research that would study, among other things, the tensions that pit man against man, race against race and nation against nation. "Our nation's future," the president of the University of Hawaii pointed out in 1959, "will depend largely upon the extent to which it is successful in bringing about greater understanding between the East and the West."

Now that the people of Hawaii have all the rights and duties of mainland citizens they are in a unique position to take the lead in matters dealing with interracial unity and Asian relations.

Whatever their color or racial origin they have learned to work together and live together without being conscious that there is anything unusual in the fact. They also have acquired enough understanding and respect for the half of the world's population that faces toward Hawaii to know something of its art and cul-

[171]

New University of Hawaii Library with part-Hawaiian, Japanese and Cauca-sian students in foreground.

ture and to realize that the languages of the Far East may some-day replace traditional French and Spanish in importance. More than people elsewhere they seem to know that one of the deepest needs of mankind today is to have a feeling of kinship with the whole world.

PAU

END

APPENDIX

Some Hawaiian Words

Word	Meaning	Pronunciation
Ae	Yes	I
Aloha	Welcome, good-by, love	AL-LO'-AH
Haole	White person; foreigner	HOW'-LIH
Holoku	Gown; dress	HO'-LO-KOO
Kamaaina	One who belongs to the Islands	KAH'-MAH-AI'-NAH
Kane	Man	KAH-NAY
Kapu	Keep out; taboo	KAH-POO'
Lanai	Verandah	LAH-NIGH
Lei	Wreath of flowers	LAY'
Mahalo	Thank you	MAH-HAH-LOH
Makai	Toward the sea	MAH-KAI'
Malihini	Stranger; newcomer	MA'-LI-HEE'-NIH
Mauka	Toward the mountains	MOW'-KUH (as in how)
Pau	Done or finished	POW
Wahine	Woman	WAH-HEE'-NIH
Wikiwiki	Hurry up	WICKY-WICKY

Pronunciation of Prominent Hawaiian Place Names

Hawaii	HAH-WAI'-EE
Honolulu	HOH'-NOH-LOO'-LOO
Iolani (palace)	EE-OH-LAH'-NEE
Kamehameha	KA-MEH'-HAH-MEH'-HAH
Kauai (island)	KOW'-AI
Kealakekua (bay)	KEH-AH'-LAH-KEH-KOO'-AH
Kilauea (active crater)	KI-LAH'-EH'-A
Maui (island)	MAW'-EE
Mauna Loa (active volcano)	MAW'-NAH-LO'-A
Molokai (island)	MOH'-LOH-KAI
Niihau (island)	NEE-HAU'
Oahu (island)	OH-AH'-HOO

[174]

Meaning of Some Hawaiian Place Names

Haleakala	House of the sun
Hamakua	The back of the island
Hanalei	Wreath making
Honolulu	Fair haven
Kailua	Two currents of the sea
Kealakekua	Path of the gods
Kilauea	Rising smoke cloud
Kona	Leeward side
Koolau	Windward side
Mauna Kea	White mountain
Mauna Loa	Long mountain
Oahu	Gathering place
Waikiki	Spurting water

Festivals and Special Days

January 17 through February 13—The Narcissus Festival: A New Year celebration by the Chinese community.

End of Febuary—Ka Palapala Pageant: The University of Hawaii's annual beauty contest in which seven queens are chosen to represent each of seven nationalities.

March 3—Japanese Girls' Day: Programs of Japanese music, flower arrangement, kimono display and exhibits of Japanese dolls to honor the birth and happiness of daughters.

March 15 to mid-April—Cherry Blossom Festival: A ten-day festival of Japanese sports, tea ceremonies, folk dancing and the selection of the state's most attractive girl of Japanese ancestry.

March 26—Kuhio Day: A state holiday observed by school programs and special ceremonies by Hawaiian societies to honor the birthday anniversary of Prince Kuhio, first delegate to Congress from Hawaii.

First Sunday in April—Wesak Day: Widely celebrated as the anniversary of Buddha's birthday. Sunrise ceremonies followed by ritualistic and modern Oriental dances.

Easter sunrise services: Held under a giant cross at the towering Punchbowl Crater which overlooks the city of Honolulu.

[175]

In April young girls of Japanese ancestry don traditional robes and vie for the honor of being queen of the annual Cherry Blossom Festival.

May 1—Lei Day: A day dedicated to the lei as a symbol of Hawaiian hospitality. Pageants are held on all the main islands with queen and flower contests. The Lei Day queen is dressed in white and wears white crown-flower leis or cream-colored pikake leis. A queen has seven attendants, one princess for each of the islands. Each princess wears a holoku the color of her home island and a lei of her island's official flower.

May 5—Boys' Day: Japanese families honor their sons. Huge paper-and-bamboo carp kites are flown.

June 11—Kamehameha Day: Honors the great King Kamehameha I and his descendants who ruled Hawaii for a century before its annexation to the United States. This is one of the Islands' most beloved festivals. The luaus (feasts), pageants and song festivals usually last for four days.

July through August—Bon Dances: Every weekend large groups of Japanese Bon dancers honor the dead with joy and dancing because it is believed they have entered paradise.

July—Japanese Weavers' Festival (Tanabata Matsuri): Perpetuates an ancient festival that dates back three thousand years with a colorful parade and weavers' dances.

September—Chinese Moon Festival: Based on the lunar calendar, this is usually celebrated in September. The festival honors the Emperor Ming-huang who visited paradise amid a garden of beautiful maidens. There is much feasting, with moon-cake displays and offerings of candy, flowers and cakes in Chinese homes, shops and temples.

Mid-October through mid-November—Aloha Week: This largest of all Hawaiian festivals is celebrated with luaus, balls, pageantry, street dancing, hula festivals and parades.

Late November to December—International Surfing Championships at Makaha on Oahu: Thousands of people crowd the beaches to watch surfers perform in one of the world's top sporting events.

December—Bodhi Day: Anniversary of the enlightenment of Buddha and the establishment of Buddhism as a world religion is celebrated on the Sunday closest to December 7.

*December 25—*Christmas is observed with "Santa" arriving on a surfboard.

APPENDIX

Land and Population

The Hawaiian Archipelago is a group of islands, reefs and shoals reaching from southeast to northwest for a distance of sixteen hundred miles. Seven of the largest islands at the southernmost end of the archipelago are populated and comprise a total land area of 6,390 square miles. The population of Hawaii in 1959 was 626,000, including 40,975 members of the American military establishment.

Island	1959 Population Figures	Land Area
Hawaii	62,464	4,030 square miles
Kauai	28,035	555 ″ ″
Lanai	2,267	141 ″ ″
Maui	36,600	728 ″ ″
Molokai	5,506	260 ″ ″
Niihau	243	72 ″ ″
Oahu	449,910	604 ″ ″

Time

Time in Hawaii is two hours earlier than Pacific Standard Time and five hours earlier than Eastern Standard Time.

Hawaiian Monarchs

	Birth	Death
Kamehameha I	1758	May 8, 1819
Kamehameha II	1799	July 14, 1824
Kamehameha III	March 17, 1814	December 15, 1854
Kamehameha IV	February 9, 1834	November 30, 1863
Kamehameha V	December 11, 1830	December 11, 1872
William C. Lunalilo	January 31, 1835	February 3, 1874
David Kalakaua	November 16, 1836	January 20, 1891
Liliuokalani	September 2, 1838	November 11, 1917

INDEX

INDEX

BIOGRAPHICAL NOTE

Charles Borden has written this book out of his wide experience in the islands and his deep interest in the people of Hawaii. He has spent twenty years as a writer, explorer, engineer and master mariner in the South Pacific, has sailed twice around the Horn and many times from Tahiti to Hawaii over the path that the early Polynesian navigators are believed to have taken.

Borden first became interested in Captain Cook, the discoverer of Hawaii, when his small skiff was swamped in a stiff blow at Waimea, Kauai, the spot where Captain Cook first landed. He has anchored in all of the small bays and harbors of Hawaii's main islands, has slept more than once in the crater of Haleakala and has spent many weeks exploring such little-known places as Waipio on Hawaii and the remote Pelekuna and Wailua valleys on rugged Molokai.

In *Hawaii—Fiftieth State* the author has combined extensive research with the latest up-to-the-minute facts. As a life member of the Polynesian Society (an organization devoted to the anthropology, ethnology and history of the Polynesian race) he has had access to authoritative material. Much information was obtained at first hand from a large circle of Island friends and from others he has known there, among them harbormasters, fishermen, bird-watchers, mountain rangers, and plantation superintendents.

"Next to the sea," he once told a friend, "I love island landfalls. Take Kauhako Bay on the Kona Coast of Hawaii, Honomanu Bay on Maui or Nawiliwili over on Kauai—each is a sailor's paradise with a safe anchorage and unspoiled beauty that is best seen from the deck of a sailboat."

Borden now lives in California, on the tip of a point of land a thousand feet out in the Pacific Ocean, and divides his time between writing and offshore cruising in his seagoing sloop Confucius III.